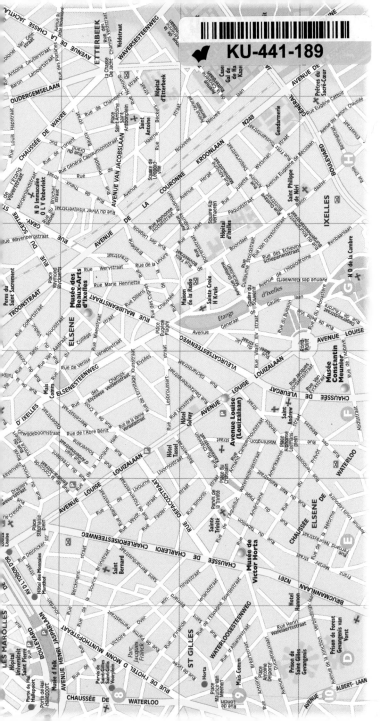

CITYPACK TOP 25
Brussels and Bruges

ANTHONY SATTIN AND SYLVIE FRANQUET

If you have any comments
or suggestions for this guide
you can contact the editor at
Citypack@theAA.com

AA Publishing
Find out more about AA Publishing and the wide
range of services the AA provides by visiting our
website at www.theAA.com/travel

How to Use This Book

KEY TO SYMBOLS

➕ Map reference to the accompanying fold-out map

✉ Address

☎ Telephone number

🕐 Opening/closing times

🍴 Restaurant or café

🚃 Nearest rail station

Ⓜ Nearest Metro station

🚌 Nearest bus route

⛴ Nearest riverboat or ferry stop

♿ Facilities for visitors with disabilities

❓ Other practical information

▷ Further information

ℹ Tourist information

✋ Admission charges: Expensive (over €8), Moderate (€4–€8) and Inexpensive (€4 or less)

★ Major Sight   ★ Minor Sight

👣 Walks   🚍 Excursions

🛍 Shops   🍴 Restaurants

🎵 Entertainment and Nightlife

🔀 Nearby attractions

This guide is divided into four sections

• **Essential Brussels and Bruges:** an introduction to the cities and tips on making the most of your stay.

• **Brussels and Bruges by Area:** we've recommended the best sights, shops, entertainment venues, nightlife and restaurants in each city. Suggested walks help you to explore on foot.

• **Where to Stay:** the best hotels, whether you're looking for luxury, budget or something in between.

• **Need to Know:** the info you need to make your trip run smoothly, including getting about by public transport, weather tips, emergency phone numbers and useful websites.

Navigation In the Brussels and Bruges by Area chapter, we've given each area its own colour, which is also used on the locator maps throughout the book and the map on the inside front cover.

Maps The fold-out map accompanying this book has comprehensive street plans of Brussels and Bruges. The grid on this fold-out map is the same as the grid on the locator maps within the book. We've given grid references within the book for each sight and listing.

Contents

CONTENTS

Introducing Brussels and Bruges

Brussels and Bruges represent the twin identities of contemporary Belgium. Brussels is the larger, busier city—and Europe's political capital. Bruges, in Flanders, is one of Europe's best-preserved medieval cities and Belgium's tourist capital.

Brussels is a cosmopolitan city: The population was already divided into Flemish and French speakers, but to these are now added the babel of European languages, with English as a common denominator. Speak to anyone who has lived here for a while and they will tell you that it is a very pleasant city to be in, with its wonderful museums, splendid architecture, delightful green spaces, excellent, reasonably priced restaurants and a lively nightlife.

The heart of the city is finally being restored and revitalized. The district around the rue Dansaert, close to the Grand' Place, has become a trendy spot to live or hang out in and nearby streets such as the rue des Chartreux and the chaussée de Flandres regularly see the opening of another hip boutique or restaurant. Other areas are also undergoing a revival, as young European professionals choose to live in the gorgeous art nouveau districts of Ixelles and St.-Gilles rather than in the suburbs.

Bruges attracts more than 2.5 million visitors each year. Flemish is the local language, although most people also know enough English to communicate with visitors. The heart of the city is small and most sights are within walking distance. If you don't want to walk, do as the locals and go by bicycle. Unlike Brussels, Bruges spent the last decades trying to keep its look medieval. The Concertgebouw, which opened in 2002, was the first statement that contemporary architecture could have a place here. Now there is a desire to create a broader environment where today's artists can be inspired by the city's rich past.

Facts + Figures

- **Brussels is the world's second-greenest capital, with 13.8 per cent of the city being green space.**
- **Bruges was European City of Culture in 2002.**
- **More than 150 monuments in Bruges have been protected.**

BRUSSELS' DISTRICTS

The heart of Brussels is enclosed by the 'Petit Ring', which more-or-less follows the 14th-century city walls. The Lower Town, near the Grand' Place, is where the working classes lived. Now fashionable, it has great restaurants and bars. The French-speaking upper classes lived, and many still do, on the hill, the Upper Town. This area has a lot of grand buildings.

CITY OF BRIDGES

No name is more appropriate than *Brugge*, Flemish for bridges. The city had its origins by a bridge over the canal *(reie)*, most probably the Blinde Ezelbrug (Blind Donkey Bridge). To protect the crossing, a borough was built around the bridge and the city grew around it. Bruges still counts many canals and about 80 bridges.

CITY OF BUREAUCRATS

Brussels is home not only to the national government of Belgium, but also to the separate parliaments of the country's three regions: Flanders, Brussels and Wallonia. It also houses the European parliament and the headquarters of NATO. The European Union employs around 30,000 people in the city and requires a huge diplomatic presence.

A Short Stay in Brussels and Bruges

DAY 1   Brussels

Morning Start the day early at the **Grand' Place** (▷ 26), admiring all the superb Gothic façades as well as the tower of the **Hôtel de Ville** (▷ 25). Rub the bronze plaque of Charles Buls, just off the square, for good luck and continue to **Manneken Pis** (▷ 28). Stroll along the **rue Antoine Dansaert** (▷ St.-Géry and Ste.-Catherine, 37) to get familiar with Belgian fashion and stop for some oysters and a glass of white wine from the stall on **place Ste.-Catherine** (▷ 37). Check out the newest space for contemporary art, the **Elektriciteitscentrale** (▷ 36).

Lunch Have a *Bruxellois'* lunch at one of the many restaurants on the Vlaamsche Steenweg, particularly **Viva M'Boma** (▷ 46) or at **Vismet** (▷ 46) for the freshest fish and seafood.

Afternoon Head for the **Sablon** (▷ 34) and enjoy a coffee on a heated terrace, before a serious dip into both old and modern art at the **Musées d'Art Ancien et Moderne** (▷ 29–31), founded by Napoleon in 1801. Browse around in the antiques shops or take in another museum if you can. The wonderful **Musée des Instruments de Musique** (▷ 32) is a good choice—the collection of musical instruments here is one of the most important of its kind in the world and it has great views from its roof terrace. End the afternoon with a stroll through the **Parc de Bruxelles** (▷ 33), once the hunting ground of Belgian kings and now a haven for *Bruxellois* and visitors alike, with its tree-lined avenues and fountain.

Dinner See **the Grand' Place** (▷ 26) by night, walk through the **Galeries St.-Hubert** (▷ 41) and eat in a typical Brussels' brasserie: the **Taverne du Passage**, **Vincent** or the grander **Belgaqueen** (▷ all 44–46). After dinner have a nightcap at one of the bars on **place St.-Géry** (▷ 37) or at **l'Archiduc** (▷ 42).

DAY 2 Bruges

Morning Start the day with a delicious breakfast at one of Bruges' top bakeries, **Servaas Van Mullem** (▷ 89). Walk over to the **Markt** (▷ 76), taking in the impressive Belfry, rising 83m (272ft) above the town. If it is a clear day, climb up for sweeping views over the city and surrounding countryside. Back down again, a narrow street leads to the even more perfect square of **Burg** (▷ 68), with the fine Gothic façade of the Town Hall and the **Heilig Bloedbasiliek** (▷ 83), where a service for the Adoration of the Holy Blood still takes place every Friday morning. Pass the **Vismarkt** (▷ 86) and walk along de Dijver to the **Groeninge Museum** (▷ 72), with its superb collection of Flemish Primitives.

Lunch Have a typical Belgian lunch at **Den Dijver** (▷ 91), which serves traditional dishes cooked with beer.

Afternoon Continue to the **Begijnhof** (▷ 66) and enjoy the tranquillity of the nearby Lac d'Amour (Lovers' Lake). Walk through the small alleys to the old **St.-Janshospitaal** (▷ 80), an interesting building in itself, which houses a fine collection of Hans Memling's paintings. Opposite the medieval hospice rises the large brick tower of the **Onze-Lieve-Vrouwekerk** (▷ 78), with Michelangelo's statue of *Madonna and Child* and other treasures. Stroll through the garden to the **Gruuthuse Museum** (▷ 74) next door. If you have any time left, take a **canal cruise** (▷ 70), starting from just opposite the museum, or ride a *calèche* (horse-drawn carriage) through town from the Burg.

Dinner If you reserve well in advance, you can enjoy dinner at **De Karmeliet** (▷ 92), ones of Bruges' best restaurants. If not, try the romantic setting of **Chez Olivier** (▷ 91). After dinner, you can work off the calories by strolling along the well-lit canals.

Top 25

► ► ► BRUSSELS

Centre Belge de la Bande Dessinée ▷ 24
A must-see for comic strip *afficionados*.

Le Cinquantenaire ▷ 50–51 Museums, auto exhibitions and monuments are all here, in one place.

Grand' Place ▷ 26–27
Admire the imposing mix of architectural brilliance in Brussels' famous square.

De Vesten en Poorten ▷ 82 These city fortifications have protected Bruges for more than 600 years.

St.-Janshospitaal en Memling Museum ▷ 80–81 Hans Memling's art works, housed in an ancient hospice.

Onze-Lieve-Vrouwekerk ▷ 78–79 Magnificent 13th-century church with important medieval art.

Markt ▷ 76–77 Since the 13th century this market square has been central to Bruges' activities.

Kathedraal St.-Salvator ▷ 75 A 13th-century place of worship containing sculptures and art.

Gruuthuse Museum ▷ 74 A glorious medieval palace with an interesting museum.

Groeninge Museum ▷ 72–73 Flemish art from the 15th century to today.

Damme ▷ 96–97 Just 6.5km (4 miles) outside Bruges, this lovely little town is worth a visit.

Chocolate Museum ▷ 71 Learn all there is to know about chocolate, and then taste the product.

These pages are a quick guide to the Top 25 sights, described in more detail later. Here they are listed alphabetically, starting with the sights in Brussels and followed by those in Bruges. The tinted background shows which area each sight is in.

Heysel ▷ 98–99
Home of the 1958 World Exhibition, with its Atomium now shiny again.

Hôtel de Ville ▷ 25
Brussels has the most elegant of all Belgium's Gothic town halls.

Manneken Pis ▷ 28
Brussels' diminutive bronze statue of a small boy continues to draw crowds.

Musée d'Art Ancien ▷ 30–31 Don't miss the classical art housed here.

Musée d'Art Moderne ▷ 29 Home to modern Belgian art.

Musée des Instruments de Musique ▷ 32 See musical instruments from across the globe.

Musée Royale de l'Afrique Centrale ▷ 100–101 A fascinating collection of ethnographic objects from Central Africa.

Musée de Victor Horta ▷ 52–53 Art nouveau at its absolute best is on show at Horta's former home.

Place Royale ▷ 33 An elegant neoclassical square overlooked by imposing palaces and monuments.

Le Sablon ▷ 34 Sit and people-watch on the terraces of this delightful square.

KOEKELBERG

MOLENBEEK

ST JEAN

**Heysel
Heizel**

BassinVergote
Vergotedok

Parc
Max-
millen-
park

**CENTRAL BRUSSELS
21–46**

Jardin Botanique
Kruidtuin Gent

Parc
Albert J-
park

Parc
Josaphat-
park

SCHAERBEEK

ST JOSSE

ST JOOST

TEN NODE

**Centre Belge
da la Bande
Dessinée**

**Grand' Place
(Grote Markt)**

**Hôtel de
Ville**

Manneken Pis

Parc de Bruxelles
Park van Brussel

**Musée des Instruments
de Musique**

**SOUTH
BRUSSELS
47–62**

**Musée d'Art
Moderne**

LE
SABLON

BRUSSEL

LES
MAROLLES

Place Royal

**Musée
d'Art Ancien**

Parc d'Egmont
Egmonttuinen

Parc Léopold
Léopoldspark

ELSENE

**Le
Cinquantenaire**
Jubelpark

ETTERBEEK

ST GILLIS

ST GILLES

Parc
Jacques
Franck

**Musée de
Victor Horta**

ELSENE

Parc de Forest
Park van Vorst

Parc Duden
Dudenpark

FOREST VORST

Parc
Brugmann-
park

Parc
Montjoie-
park

UKKEL

Etangs
d'Ixelles

IXELLES

**Musée Royale
de l'Afrique
Centrale**

Cimetière d'Ixelles
Begraafplaats van Elsene

BRUSSEL

Bois de
la Cambre

Canal Cruise ▷ 70 A wonderful way to explore the city known as the 'Venice of the North'.

Burg ▷ 68–69 A medieval square bounded on all sides by impressive buildings of historical note.

Begijnhof ▷ 66–67 This pretty square of houses was home to an all-female pious community.

BRUGES ◄ ◄ ◄

9

Shopping

An obvious souvenir from Belgium, if not a lasting one, is food. Belgium is known for its plain chocolate, which contains only the best cocoa and a very high proportion of it.

A Chocoholic's Dream Destination
Belgians are serious about their chocolate, as is obvious from the number of shops devoted to chocolate in its many shapes, shades and tastes. You can buy good chocolate bars, such as Côte d'Or, in supermarkets, but it's the handmade chocolates and pralines that stand out. Prices are generally low, except for chocolates by the high priest of chocolate, Pierre Marcolini, or by the internationally renowned Godiva (both ▷ 41). Do as the Belgians and look for smaller patisseries that make their own, including Speghelaere (▷ 89) and Depla (▷ 88) in Bruges and Mary's (▷ 41) in Brussels.

The Way the Cookie Crumbles
Equally delicious are Belgian cookies such as *speculoos* (slightly spicy biscuits), *pain Grècque* (a light biscuit with sugar), *amandelbrood* (butter biscuit with shaved almonds) and *peperkoek* (a cake with cinnamon and candied fruits). *Destrooper* is a good brand and is stocked in supermarkets.

TRENDY SHOPPING

Brussels is slowly taking over from Antwerp as Belgium's fashion capital. The Brussels tourist office, on Grand' Place, publishes a useful brochure called *Fashionable Districts* that reveals the obvious fashion districts as well as upcoming places such as St.-Gilles, rue du Bailli and place du Châtelain. In the old Saint Boniface quarter you'll find new designers and stores as well as hip bars and restaurants. Most Belgian designers, including Walter Van Bierendonck, Ann Demeulemeester, Dries Van Noten, Dirk Bikkembery, Veronique Branquinho and Chris Mestdagh, are available at the Stijl (▷ 41), the store that is the grand temple of Belgian fashion. These designers produce accessible avant-garde fashion, while designers such as Chine (▷ 57) and Olivier Strelli (▷ 58) produce more commercial clothes.

Liquid Refreshment

Beer is another good buy, with 700 labels to choose from. Every bar has a beer menu, so you might want to try a few varieties before stocking up. Larger supermarkets have a good selection of beers, and beer shops can be found in tourist areas in both cities.

Lace, Tapestry and Fashion

Belgium was famous in the Middle Ages for its tapestry and exquisite lace, and there is still plenty of it for sale, although very little is now handmade in Belgium and what you can find is usually very pricey. Belgian fashion designers are currently enjoying worldwide success, so take a closer look at their work in Brussels, particularly in and around the rue Antoine Dansaert. Local designers such as Dries Van Noten, Martin Margiela and Veronique Branquinho create innovative designs based on Belgian traditions.

Art and Comics

Art galleries are all over Brussels—for details obtain a copy of the brochure *Art Brussels* from the tourist office. Many shops specialize in comic books, but none so much as the Tintin shops (▷ 40, 89). Here you can choose from a selection of Tintin books, collectables, clothes, towels and even wallpaper.

SHOPPING DISTRICTS

The main shopping streets in Bruges are Geldmuntstraat-Noordzandstraat and Steenstraat-Zuidzandstraat. In Brussels, the main shopping street, rue Neuve, has all the international high-street brands and the large shopping mall City 2. The Galeries St.-Hubert (▷ 41) has good traditional shops focusing on design, books, fashion and chocolates. Avenue Louise is Brussels' traditional shopping area, with everything from Chanel to the Belgian designer Olivier Strelli (▷ 58). The fashionable place to shop, however, is the area around rue Antoine Dansaert (▷ 37, St.-Géry), which has the best shoe shops in Brussels and shops of new designers.

Shopping by Theme

Whether you're looking for a department store, a quirky boutique, or something in between, you'll find it all in Brussels and Bruges. On this page shops are listed by theme. For a more detailed write-up, see the individual listings in Brussels and Bruges by Area.

ANTIQUES AND SECOND-HAND GOODS

BRUSSELS
Antik Blaes (▷ 40)
Galerie Vanderkindere (▷ 57)
K. Grusenmeyer (▷ 41)
Look 50 (▷ 58)

BRUGES
Yannick de Hondt (▷ 89)

BELGIAN CHOCOLATE

BRUSSELS
A. M. Sweet (▷ 40)
Godiva (▷ 41)
Mary's (▷ 41)
Pierre Marcolini (▷ 41)

BRUGES
Depla (▷ 88)
Servaas van Mullem (▷ 89)
Speghelaere (▷ 89)

BOOKS

BRUSSELS
Anticyclone des Açores (▷ 40)
Brüsel (▷ 40)
FNAC (▷ 41)

BRUGES
Raaklijn (▷ 89)
De Reyghere (▷ 89)
De Striep (▷ 89)

FASHION

BRUSSELS
Chine Collection (▷ 57)
Christophe Coppens (▷ 40)
Greta Marta (▷ 57)
Ideb Lifestore (▷ 58)
Martin Margiela (▷ 41)
Olivier Strelli (▷ 58)
Stilj (▷ 41)

BRUGES
L'Heroïone (▷ 88)
Olivier Strelli (▷ 89

FOOD

BRUSSELS
Au Suisse (▷ 40)
Dandoy (▷ 40)
Fromagerie Maison Baguette-Gaspard (▷ 57)
Marché Place du Châtelain (▷ 58)
Patisserie Wittamer (▷ 41)

BRUGES
Deldycke (▷ 88)
Diksmuids Boterhuis (▷ 88)
Malesherbes (▷ 89)

CRAFTS AND GIFTS

BRUSSELS
Au Grand Rasoir (▷ 40)
AXL (▷ 57)
La Boutique de Tintin (▷ 40)

Christa Reniers (▷ 40)
Plaizier (▷ 41)
Les Précieuses (▷ 58)
Senteurs d'Ailleurs (▷ 58)

BRUGES
'T Apostelientje (▷ 88)
Bazar Bizar (▷ 88)
Brugs Diamanthuis (▷ 88)
Dille & Kamille (▷ 88)
Gruuthuse Lace Shop (▷ 88)
Kantcentrum (Lace Centre) (▷ 89)
Tintin Shop (▷ 89)

OFFBEAT AND UNUSUAL

BRUSSELS
Art Deco 1920–1940 (▷ 57)
Beer Mania (▷ 57)
Le Bonheur-Epicerie Audiovisuelle (▷ 40)
Le Dépôt (▷ 57)
Espace Bizarre (▷ 41)
Serneels (▷ 58)

BRUGES
Hoet Optiek (▷ 88)
Iki (▷ 88)
The Old Curiosity Shop (▷ 89)
Rombaux (▷ 89)

Brussels and Bruges by Night

The Belgian joke that there's a bar on every corner can't be far from the truth. What's more, licensing laws permit them to stay open as long as they like—often until dawn.

Enjoying a Drink

The bar scene is lively in both cities, as this is what locals do when they go out at night. Even if they go out for dinner or to a show, they still end up having a beer in a bar. The pace of drinking is usually slow but steady, making it easier to keep going all night. In Brussels you can start on the Grand' Place, where the view comes at a price. Nearby there are trendy bars around the place St.-Géry and rue Marché au Charbon, as well as pricier establishments around Le Sablon. Look in Les Marolles or St.-Gilles for distinctively *Bruxellois* cafés, stained dark from decades of tobacco smoke. For jazz clubs and wine bars, try Ixelles.

An Evening Stroll

In Brussels, head for the Grand' Place, beautifully floodlit at night. In Bruges, the liveliest areas are the Eiermarkt and t'Zand.

Outdoor Living

In summer, Belgians spend long evenings sitting on café terraces chatting. The best in Brussels include Le Roy d'Espagne, La Lunette, Le Falstaff (▷ 45) and the café terraces on the place du Grand Sablon. In Bruges, most people head for cafés in the Eiermarkt and t'Zand.

WHAT'S ON

The English-language weekly *The Bulletin* has a 'What's On' supplement, or pick up one of the free city guides, like *Agenda* or *Rif Raf* (www.rifraf.be) in Brussels, or *Exit* in Bruges. All have entertainment listings in Flemish or French, but it's pretty easy to identify what's going on. In Brussels, tickets to events can be bought from FNAC (in City 2, rue Neuve ☎ 0900 00600), the tourist office on the Grand' Place or the venue; in Bruges from the tourist office in Concertgebouw, on t'Zand (☎ 050 476 999).

Eating Out

Belgians love to eat and they do it well. Brussels and Bruges have no shortage of excellent restaurants offering Belgian and international fare, prepared with fresh ingredients and served in simple but convivial surroundings. This is true for most eateries, from the simple bistro to the ultimate palace of haute cuisine.

Belgian Dishes

Contrary to popular belief, there is more to Belgian food than *moules frites*. *Waterzooi* is a little-known national dish, a delicate green stew of fish or chicken with leeks, parsley and cream. Plain but delicious, *stoemp* is potatoes mashed with vegetables, often served with sausages. *Carbonnade flamande* is beef braised in beer with carrots and thyme, and *lapin à la gueuze* is rabbit stewed in gueuze beer with prunes. *Anguilles au vert/paling in het groen* (river eels in green sauce) is another popular dish. A real treat are Belgian waffles, eaten with icing sugar, whipped cream or fruit.

Vegetarian Choices

Belgians like their meat, but options are available for vegetarians. For those who eat it, there is always plenty of fish on the menu. Salads are a popular choice for lunch and vegetarians will find plenty of meat-free dishes in ethnic restaurants, as well as in some specifically vegetarian restaurants. For vegetarian restaurant suggestions in Brussels ▷ 62. In Bruges, try Lotus (▷ 92).

FRITES, FRITES, FRITES

Belgium claims the best fries in the world. The secret of their *frites* is that they are fried twice and thrown into the air to get rid of the extra oil. Every Belgian has a preferred *frietkot* or *friture*, but most agree that Maison Antoine (▷ 62), on the place Jourdan in Brussels, and La Barrière St.-Gilles, at 3 chaussée d'Alsemberg in St.-Gilles, are the best. In Bruges, have a cone of piping hot *frites* from the *frietkot* on the Markt.

Restaurants by Cuisine

There are restaurants to suit all tastes and budgets in Brussels and Bruges. On this page they are listed by cuisine. For a more detailed description of each restaurant, see Brussels and Bruges by Area.

BEST DINING

BRUSSELS
La Belle Maraîchère
  (▷ 44)
Chez Marie (▷ 60)
Claude Dupont (▷ 44)
Comme Chez Soi (▷ 45)
Domaine de Lintillac
  (▷ 45)
La Manufacture (▷ 45)
La Quincaillerie (▷ 62)
Resource (▷ 46)
Vismet (▷ 46)
Viva M'Boma (▷ 46)

BRUGES
Den Braamberg (▷ 91)
Den Gouden Harynck
  (▷ 92)
De Karmeliet (▷ 92)

BELGIAN AND BRASSERIES

BRUSSELS
L'Amadeus (▷ 60)
Belgaqueen (▷ 44)
Belgo Belge (▷ 60)
Le Framboisier Doré
  (sorbets; ▷ 62)
Le Pain Quotidien/Het
  Dagelyjks Brood (▷ 46)
Taverne du Passage
  (▷ 46)
De Ultieme Hallucinatie
  (▷ 46)
L'Ultime Atome (▷ 62)
Vincent (▷ 46)

BRUGES
Breydel-de-Coninc (▷ 91)
Cafedraal (▷ 91)
Chez Olivier (▷ 91)
Christophe (▷ 91)
Den Dijver (▷ 91)
Lotus (▷ 92)
T'Zonneke (▷ 92)

INTERNATIONAL CUISINE

BRUSSELS
Aux Mille et Une Nuits
  (Tunisian; ▷ 60)
Bocconi (Italian; ▷ 44)
Bonsoir Clara
  (Mediterranean; ▷ 44)
Comocomo (tapas; ▷ 44)
Eat & Love
  (Vietnamese/Thai; ▷ 60)
Divino (Italian; ▷ 45)
Le Fils de Jules
  (Basque; ▷ 60)
Gioconda Store Convivio
  (Italian; ▷ 62)
Le Hasard des Choses
  (Mediterranean; ▷ 62)
L'Horlage du Sud
  (West African; ▷ 62)
Kasbah (Moroccan; ▷ 45)

Little Asia
  (Vietnamese; ▷ 45)
Sahbaz (Turkish; ▷ 46)
Tagawa (Japanese; ▷ 62)

BRUGES
Ryad (Moroccan; ▷ 92)
Tanuki (Japanese; ▷ 92)
Rock Fort
  (Mediterranean; ▷ 92)

BARS AND CAFÉS

BRUSSELS
Brasserie Verschueren
  (▷ 60)
Café Belga (▷ 60)
Le Cercle des Voyageurs
  (▷ 44)
Daringman (▷ 45)
Le Falstaff (▷ 45)

BRUGES
'T Brugs Beertje (▷ 91)
Doowop (▷ 90)
L'Estaminet (▷ 91)
Est Wijnbar (▷ 91)
Heer Halewijn (▷ 92)
Oude Vlissinghe (▷ 92)
De Republiek (▷ 92)

If You Like...

However you'd like to spend your time in Brussels and Bruges, these top suggestions should help you tailor your ideal visit. Each sight or listing has a fuller write-up in Brussels and Bruges by Area.

A LAZY MORNING

Immerse yourself in the junk market at place du Jeu de Balle in the Marolles district of Brussels (▷ 36) on a Sunday morning.

Linger over a coffee and a delicious pastry at Le Pain Quotidien (▷ 46) in Brussels.

Walk through the park that covers the old city walls around Bruges (▷ 82).

ART NOUVEAU ARCHITECTURE

Head for Victor Horta's own house in Brussels, now the splendid Horta Museum (▷ 52).

Rent a bicycle and cycle past Brussels' many art nouveau monuments (▷ 56).

Visit a museum: The Musée des Instruments de Musique (▷ 32) or the Comic Strip Museum (▷ 24) are both superb examples of Brussels' art nouveau architecture.

Façade of the Musée des Instruments de Musique (above) and the Marolles flea market (top)

SHOPPING SPREES

For Belgian fashion head for Stijl (▷ 41) and other stores in Brussels' rue Antoine Dansaert and the surrounding area.

For designer labels Brussels' avenue Louise is your ticket to paradise.

For antiques visit the weekend antiques market on the Sablon (▷ 34).

ROMANTIC EVENING STROLLS

Take in the Grand' Place, spectacularly lit at night (▷ 26).

Walk along the canals in the heart of Bruges (▷ 70).

Take an evening stroll in Bruges' Markt (right)

Don't forget to sample some delicious Belgian chocolates (below)

CHOCOLATES

Visit the high temple of chocolate, Pierre Marcolini's grand and stylish shop (▷ 41) on the Sablon in Brussels.

Learn about the history of chocolate and how the Belgian pralines are made at Bruges' Chocolate Museum (▷ 71).

Taste the best chocolates, hand-made in small patisseries such as Speghelaere (▷ 89) in Bruges and Mary's (▷ 41) in Brussels.

CULTURE TRAILS

Admire the Flemish Primitives in all their glory at Bruges' Groeninge Museum (▷ 72–73) and Hans Memling Museum (▷ 80–81) or Brussels' Musée d'Art Ancien (▷ 30–31).

Take time to view the façades of each house on the Grand' Place in Brussels (▷ 26).

Hitch a ride on one of the canal boats in Bruges (▷ 70) to understand why the city is known as 'Venice of the North'.

BELGIAN CUISINE

The flower market on Grand' Place (above) and a boat on Bruges' Groenerei (above middle)

Try the exquisite offal dishes at one of Brussels' most acclaimed restaurants, Viva M'Boma (▷ 46).

Watch the waiter prepare a spectacular Steak Tartare (raw beef) at your table at Vincent (▷ 46).

Enjoy the ultimate Belgian culinary delights at the three-Michelin-star Comme Chez Soi (▷ 45), but reserve well in advance.

Pierre Wynants (left) demonstrates his skills at Comme Chez Soi

STAYING IN LUXURY

Rocco Forte's Amigo Hotel (▷ 112) hits the
right spot—a stylish, luxurious hotel with
immaculate service, located right
next to Brussels' Grand' Place.
The Hyatt Regency in Brussels
(▷ 112) offers stylish yet homey
luxury and is close to the shops.
The Relais Ravenstein in Bruges
(▷ 112) has a fine canalside location
and 15 well-designed suites with
Jacuzzi and flat-screen televisions.

INTIMATE HOTELS

De Orangerie (▷ 112) is one
of Bruges' most romantic
hotels, in a 15th-century
convent next to one of the
city's most beautiful canals.
Le Dixseptième, in a great location in Brussels
(▷ 112), offers charming rooms in a beautifully
restored 17th-century building.

*Enjoy opera at Théatre
Royal de la Monnaie
(above) or rides at Six
Flags Belgium (below)*

OPERA AND DANCE

Witness world-class opera and marvel at the
opulent décor at the national opera house of
Théâtre Royal de la Monnaie (▷ 37), in Brussels.
Watch and hear local and international dance
and music at Bruges' Concertgebouw (▷ 83), the
city's 21st-century landmark.

KEEPING THE KIDS HAPPY

Buy kids' fashion by mainly Belgian
designers from the kids' store of Stijl
(▷ 41), Kat en Muis, at 34 rue
Antoine Dansaert in Brussels.
Brave the rides at the theme park
Six Flags Belgium (▷ 106).
Watch the dolphins and enjoy the
fairground at the Boudewijn Seapark
in Bruges (▷ 102).

Brussels and Bruges by Area

CENTRAL BRUSSELS

SOUTH BRUSSELS

BRUGES

FARTHER AFIELD

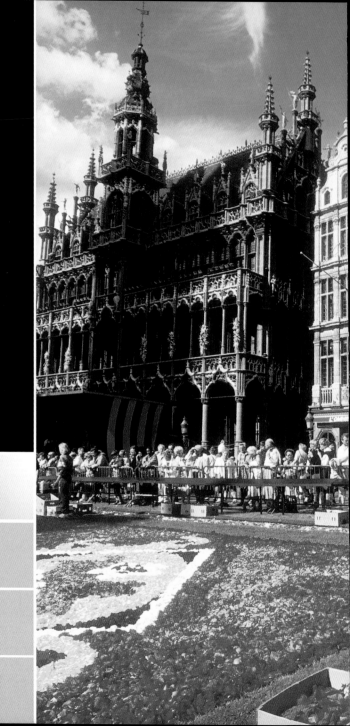

The Lower Town, around the Grand' Place, is the historical heart of Brussels. The Upper Town, on a steep hill, is home to royalty, state institutions and art museums.

AV DU BD
BOLWERKLN
Rogier BOULEVARD DU JARDIN BOTANIQUE

Adolphe Malaan

City 2

Nieuwstraat

Rue de la Blanchisserie

N D du Finistère

Clinique
Saint Jean

Institute et
Fac Saint Louis

Rue

aux Choux

Broekstraat

Congrès
Kongres

Cité
Admini-
strative

Botanique
Kruidtuin

BOULEVARD BISCHOFFSHEIM

Musée
du Jouet

Straat

Place des
Barricades

Rue du Nord

Rue des
Boiteux

Rue des
Comédiens

Marais

Centre Belge
da la Bande
Dessinée

BD DE BERLAIMONT

Place du
Congrès

Rue du
Gouvernement
Provisoire

Colonne du
Congrès

Place de la
Liberté

Konings

Rue de ligne

Rue du Congrès

Rue de
la Presse

R2D

Rue d'Arenberg

Rue de la
Montagne

BD DE L'IMPERATRICE

Rue de
Loxum

Banque
Nationale
Bank

Cathédrale
St-Michel et
Ste-Gudule

Place et Parvis
Saint Gudule

Rue des Colonies

Royale

Rue de l'Enseignement

Cirque
Royale

Rue de Louvain

Straat

R2D

Rue de la Loi

Palais de la
Nation

Hertog-

Gare
Centrale

BD DE GARE CENTRALE
CENTRAL STATION

Cantersteen

Rue Ravenstein

Pal des
Congrès

S G B
Ravenstein

Parc
Park

Place de la
Nation

Théâtre
Royal du Parc

LAAN

Mont
des Arts

BOZAR

Parc de Bruxelles
Park van Brussel

Ducale

REGENT-

Bibl
Royal

Musée
d'Art
Moderne

Musée des Instruments
de Musique

PLACE DE PALAIS

Rue

Palais des
Académies

Musée
d'Art
Ancien

Place
Royal

Saint
Jacques-sur-
Coudenberg

BELvue
Museum

Palais du Roi
Paleis van de
Koning

RUE DUCALE

broeck

LA REGENCE

Cour des
Comptes

Rue de Namur

Rue Bréderodestraat

Place du
Trône

N D du
Sablon

Palais
d'Egmont

Rue des Petits Carmes

Porte de Namur
Naamsepoort

Rue du Pépin

rue de la Pépinière

BOULEVARD

Parc d'Egmont
Egmonttuinen

WATERLOOLAAN

0   250 m

0   250 yds

E   F   G

Centre Belge de la Bande Dessinée

Cheerful cartoons at the Centre Belge de la Bande Dessinée (below)

THE BASICS

www.comicscenter.net

E4

20 rue des Sables

02 219 1980

Tue–Sun 10–6. Closed Easter and some holidays

Restaurant/bar

Gare Centrale/Centraal station/de Brouckère/ Rogier

Tram 3, 23, 52, 55, 56, 81, 90, 92, 93, 94

Good

Moderate

DID YOU KNOW?

● Tintin books have been translated into 51 languages.
● The House of the Comic Strip recently opened its doors at boulevard de l'Impératrice 1 (02 502 9468, www.jije.org), with the works of Joseph Gillain, known under the pencil name of Jijé, and the young artists he helped to set up.
● Brussels has a Comic Strip Route (6km/4 miles), with the most famous characters painted on façades. A map is available from the tourist office on Grand' Place or at www.brusselsinternational.be.

'Captain Haddock: "Land Ho! Land Ho! Thundering typhoons! Land...about time, too!" Tintin: "Why?...Are we out of fuel-oil?" Haddock: "Worse than that!...We're out of whisky!!"'–Hergé's The Adventures of Tintin: The Shooting Star.

Comic strips and more comic strips Combining comic strips and art nouveau, this is one of Brussels' unusual delights. Although comic strips, or *bds* (*bandes dessinées*), were not invented in Belgium, Belgian artists took the form to new heights. The most famous of them is Hergé (Georges Rémi), with his 1929 creations Tintin and Milou (Snowy). The Museum Bookshop stocks thousands of comic strips and collectables and there is an excellent art nouveau brasserie.

Hands-on entertainment The mezzanine houses an extensive archive, a cinema and an exhibition explaining how *bds* are made. On the upper floor, sections are devoted to each of the great Belgian *bd* creators, with pages to admire as well as hands-on exhibits. The lower floor shows work by Victor Horta (▷ 52–53).

The Magazins Waucquez The collection is housed in the old Waucquez fabric store that opened in 1906. It is a masterpiece of art nouveau, designed by Victor Horta, with a sweeping staircase, glass skylights and plant motifs. The building fell into disrepair in the 1970s, but was beautifully restored in the 1990s to become a museum.

A door detail (below) and the Gothic frontage (below right) of the Hôtel de Ville

Hôtel de Ville

Had architect Jan van Ruysbroeck foreseen how much his elegant bell tower for the Hôtel de Ville would be admired today, perhaps he would not have thrown himself off it. The Town Hall itself is a Gothic masterpiece.

A work of art Flanders and Brabant have a wealth of Gothic town halls, but the Brussels Hôtel de Ville is probably the most beautiful of all. It was started in the spring of 1402; the right wing was added in 1444. The octagonal tower, 96m (315ft) high, was added later by architect Jan van Ruysbroeck and bears a gilt statue of the Archangel St. Michael. The top of the tower, 400 steps up, gives the best views over the Grand' Place. Most sculptures adorning the façade of the Town Hall are 19th-century replacements of 14th- and 15th-century originals that are now in the Musée de la Ville de Bruxelles (▶ 37). The courtyard has two 18th-century fountains against the west wall, representing Belgium's most important rivers—the Meuse (to the left) and Scheldt (right).

The Grand Staircase The Grand Staircase carries the busts of all the mayors of Brussels since Belgian independence in 1830. Count Jacques Lalaing painted the murals on the walls in 1893.

The Gothic Hall The splendid 16th-century Council Chamber is decorated with lavish 19th-century tapestries depicting the city's main guilds and crafts. There is a flourish of gilt mouldings and the oak floor is inlaid with ebony.

THE BASICS

- E5
- ✉ Grand' Place
- ☎ 02 513 8940 (tourist office)
- Guided tours only, in English; Apr–end Sep Tue, Wed 3.15pm, Sun 10.45am, 12.15pm
- Gare Centrale/Centraal Station or Bourse/Beurse
- Tram 23, 52, 55, 56, 81
- Good
- Inexpensive

HIGHLIGHTS

- Grand Staircase
- Bell tower
- Magnificent tapestries

Grand' Place

HIGHLIGHTS

- Hôtel de Ville (▷ 25)
- La Maison du Roi, now the Museé de la Ville de Bruxelles (▷ 37)
- Elegant dome of Roi d'Espagne
- Bronze plaques of Charles Buls and Everard 't Serclaes left of Hôtel de Ville, to be stroked for good luck
- No. 10 L'Arbre d'Or (Golden Tree) is the Museum of Belgian Brewers and No. 13 is the Musée du Cacao et du Chocolat

In the morning, the sun lights up the gilded Gothic, Renaissance and baroque façades of one of the world's most stunning squares. This is the unquestionable heart of Brussels.

Early days By the 11th century, the Grand' Place was already humming as a market place, and by the 13th century the first three guildhalls had been built here, for the butchers, bakers and clothmakers. The guilds were trade organizations that regulated working conditions and hours, as well as the trade outside the town. As the guilds became increasingly powerful, they even took part in a number of wars, and commanded ever higher membership fees. The guilds' might is never more palpable than when you stand in the Grand' Place. Destroyed by a French bombardment in

Clockwise from left: a regal statue crowns the Maison du Roi; horses and flagbearers take part in the vivid Ommegang pageant, as people look on; a statue tops Le Roy d'Espagne building; a group of life-size Meyboom Puppets pose for a photograph

1695 (except for the Hôtel de Ville, ▷ 25), the square was entirely rebuilt by the guilds in less than five years.

The guildhalls Each one in the Grand' Place is distinguished by statues and ornate carvings. Look for No. 5 La Louve (the She-Wolf), representing the archers' guild; No. 7 Le Renard (Fox), the haberdashers' guild; No. 9 Le Cygne (Swan), the butchers' guild, where Karl Marx and Friedrich Engels wrote the *Communist Manifesto* in 1848; Nos. 24–25 La Chaloupe d'Or (Golden Galleon), the tailors' guild; and No. 26–27 Le Pigeon, representing the painters' guild, where novelist Victor Hugo stayed in 1852. Of particular interest are Nos. 29–33, the Maison du Roi, also called the Broodhuis in Flemish; it belonged not to a king but to the bakers' guild.

THE BASICS

✚ E5
🍴 Restaurants on the square
🚇 Gare Centrale/Centraal Station or Bourse/Beurs
🚊 Tram 23, 52, 55, 56, 81
♿ Good 🆓 Free
🔁 Manneken Pis (▷ 28), Centre Belge de la Bande Dessinée (▷ 24), Musée de la Ville de Bruxelles (▷ 37)
❓ Mid-Dec Christmas fair with Christmas tree, shopping, food and concerts

Manneken Pis

TOP 25

Left to right: Europe Day celebrations; Mannekin uncovered; posing for that must-have photo

THE BASICS

☩ D5
✉ Corner of rue de l'Etuve and rue du Chènet
🚇 Gare Centrale/Centraal Station or Bourse/Beurs
🚊 Tram 23, 52, 55, 56, 81
🎫 Free
🔗 Grand' Place (▷ 26), Hôtel de Ville (▷ 25), Musée de la Ville de Bruxelles (▷ 37)
❓ For the dates when Manneken Pis is dressed up, see the sign at the statue

DID YOU KNOW?

● In 1985, feminists demanded a female version of Manneken Pis and commissioned Jeanneke Pis (BImpasse de la Fidelité, off the rue des Bouchers).
● Every 13 September Manneken Pis wears the uniform of a sergeant in the Regiment of Welsh Guards to celebrate the liberation of Brussels in 1944.

If it were not for the bus-loads of tourists who gather in front of this little fellow to have their picture taken, it would be easy to walk past him—a strange mascot for a city.

Cheeky cherub Manneken Pis, meaning 'pissing little boy', is one of Brussels' more amusing symbols. The bronze statuette, less than 60cm (2ft) high, was created by Jérôme Duquesnoy the Elder in 1619. Known then as 'Petit Julien', it has since become a legend. One story claims that the Julien on whom the statue was modelled was the son of Duke Gottfried of Lorraine; another alleges that the statue urinated on a bomb fuse to save the Town Hall from destruction.

Often vandalized The statue was kidnapped by the English in 1745, as a way of getting at the people of Brussels; two years later the French took him away. In 1817 he was stolen by a French convict and was in pieces when he was recovered. The fragments were used to make the mould for the present statue. Even now he remains a temptation: He has been removed several times by drunk or angry students.

An extravagant wardrobe The French king Louis XV gave him a richly embroidered robe and the cross of Louis XIV as reparation for the bad actions of his soldiers in 1747. Now, Manneken Pis has hundreds of costumes, which you can see in the Musée de la Ville de Bruxelles (▷ 37), a few streets away on the Grand' Place.

Discover modern Belgian art at the Musée d'Art Moderne

This museum puts modern Belgian artists in their context, and many of them shine, even among the great European stars. The venue also stages important temporary exhibitions.

20th-century Belgians Belgian artists are sometimes overlooked in preference for their other European contemporaries, so perhaps there is something symbolic in the fact that the Modern Art Museum is buried in a multi-level subterranean building. But a visit to the chronologically arranged galleries is most rewarding, and reveals some outstanding works.

Fauvists and Surrealists In the early 20th century, local artists were particularly interested by fauvism, best represented by the works of Rik Wouters, Auguste Oleffe and Léon Spilliaert, and surrealism, which grew out of the post-World War I chaos. Belgians René Magritte and Paul Delvaux are two stars of surrealism, and the museum collection includes one of Magritte's most famous paintings *The Dominion of Light*. Among the foreign artists represented here are Max Ernst, Francis Picabia, James Ensor and Oskar Kokoshka.

Other movements The lower levels show Belgian futurism, abstract art, pop art, new realism and minimal art. Particularly important here is the work of Marcel Broodthaers. A collection of works by Henri Matisse, Raoul Dufy, Picasso, Giorgio de Chirico, Marc Chagall and Dalí helps to put the Belgian artists in a wider context.

THE BASICS

www.fine-arts-museum.be

➕ E6

✉ 1–2 place Royale

☎ 02 508 3211

🕐 Tue–Sun 10–5

🍴 Cafeteria-restaurant

🚇 Gare Centrale/Centraal Station or Trône/Troon

🚌 27, 34, 38, 60, 71, 95, 96; tram 92, 93, 94

♿ Very good

💷 Moderate (free every 1st Wed of month from 1pm)

🔄 Le Sablon (▷ 34), Musée d'Art Ancien (▷ 30–31), Musée des Instruments de Musique (▷ 32), place Royale (▷ 33)

❓ Regular temporary exhibitions as well as readings and music (information from Friends of the Museum ☎ 02 511 4116)

HIGHLIGHTS

● *L'Empire des Lumières* and others, René Magritte
● *The Flautist* and *The Woman with the Yellow Necklace*, Rik Wouters
● *Skeletons Quarrelling for a Kipper*, James Ensor, 1891
● *The Public Voice* and *Pygmalion*, Paul Delvaux

CENTRAL BRUSSELS

⭐ **TOP 25**

Musée d'Art Ancien

HIGHLIGHTS

● *Landscape with the Fall of Icarus* and *The Census at Bethlehem*, Bruegel
● *The Ascent to Calvary* and *The Martyrdom of St. Lievin*, Rubens
● *Portrait of Anthony of Burgundy*, Dirk Bouts
● *La Justice d'Otton*, Dirk Bouts
● *The Scandalized Masks*, James Ensor
● *The Temptation of St. Anthony*, School of Hieronymus Bosch
● Sculpture garden next to the museum

The Museum of Old Art highlights how rich a period the 14th to 17th centuries were for Belgian art, with works by Pieter Brueghel the Elder, Rubens, the Flemish Primitives, and other European masters like Tintoretto and Rembrandt.

Museum history The Old Art Museum and the nearby Modern Art Museum (▷ 29) were founded by Napoleon in 1801 as the Museum of Brussels. The Old Art Museum is in a building constructed in 1874–80 by Leopold II's colonial architect, Alphonse Balat. It saw complete modernization in the 1980s and is now connected to the Museum of Modern Art by an underground passage.

Artistic riches The tour of the museum starts with a collection of impressive works by the Flemish

THE BASICS

www.fine-arts-museum.be

🔛 E6

✉ 3 rue de la Régence

☎ 02 508 3211

🕐 Tue–Sun 10–5

🍴 Cafeteria-restaurant

🚇 Gare Centrale/Centraal Station

🚌 20, 34, 38, 60, 71, 95, 96; tram 92, 93, 94

♿ Good

💰 Moderate (free every 1st Wed of month from 1pm)

Le Sablon (▷ 34), Musée d'Art Moderne (▷ 29), place Royale (▷ 33), Musée des Instruments de Musique (▷ 32)

❓ Regular exhibitions, music and readings (information from Friends of the Museum ☎ 02 511 4116)

Primitives. They are well represented here with works by Rogier van der Weyden, Dirk Bouts, Hieronymus Bosch, Gerard David and particularly Hans Memling. The museum's collection of the works of the Brueghels is world-class, second only to that in Vienna's Kunst-Historisches Museum. Later artists include Jacob Jordaens.

Sculpture The central Forum, on the first floor, is home to a collection of 19th-century sculptures, including works by Jan van Kessels and Rodin, while the rooms off it contain masterpieces of the Romantic and Classical movements, including paintings by Delacroix.

Sculpture garden The sculpture collection in the garden beside the museum is less well known, but is excellent and well-arranged.

Musée des Instruments de Musique

TOP 25

The museum's distinctive art nouveau façade (left); pianos on display (below)

THE BASICS

www.mim.fgov.be

➕ E6

✉ 2 rue Montagne de la Cour

☎ 02 545 0130

🕐 Tue–Fri 9.30–5, Sat, Sun 10–5

🍴 Bar and restaurant (on top floor, with summer terrace)

Ⓡ Gare Centrale/Centraal Station or Parc/Park

🚋 Tram 92, 94, 94

♿ Good

💶 Moderate; free 1st Wed of the month after 1pm

❓ Walking tours every Fri, 10.30–12, about the history of a particular instrument. Workshops in music, dance, and the making of instruments

🔗 Musée d'Art Moderne (▷ 29), Musée d'Art Ancien (▷ 30–31), place Royale (▷ 33)

DID YOU KNOW?

● Giacomo Puccini died in 1924 in a hospital near the place du Trône, in Brussels.

● Adolphe Sax, who invented the saxophone in 1846, studied at the Royal Music Conservatoire in Brussels, where Clara Schumann, Hector Berlioz, Niccolo Paganini, Richard Wagner and many others appeared.

The Museum of Musical Instruments is a pleasure to visit, both for its amazing collection and for the art nouveau architecture of its 'Old England' building.

The collection When in 1877 King Leopold II received a large number of Hindu instruments from Rajah Sourindo Mohun Tagore, and at the same time the musicologist Jean-François Fetis donated his collection to the State, it was decided to create a Museum of Musical Instruments. Since then the museum has acquired instruments from across the centuries and from all over the world. Today, with more than 7,000 instruments, one quarter of which are on display, it is one of the most important museums of its kind in the world. The bulk of the collection is European, from the Renaissance onwards. Every instrument is beautifully displayed, and some are astonishing, like the glass harmonica designed by the American inventor and statesman Benjamin Franklin (1706–90), for which both Beethoven and Mozart wrote music, or the 18th-century *pochettes*, tiny violins that violin teachers could carry in their pockets. Using a headset, you can listen to music played by the instrument at which you are looking.

Old England Building The Old England Department Store, in which the museum is housed, was designed in 1899 by Paul Saintenoy. Inspired by the British Arts and Crafts movement, he decided upon a grand art nouveau style building with cast-iron pillars, swirling wrought iron, painted floral decoration and lots of natural light.

This elegant neoclassical square is anchored by some powerful institutions: the Royal Palace, the Belgian Parliament and the Law Courts.

Symmetrical square The place Royale was built 1774–80, an enclosed rectangle made up of eight palaces joined by porticoes. At the heart stands the statue of Godefroid de Bouillon, who led the first crusade in the 11th century. The rue de la Régence links the square with the imposing Law Courts, and at the other end is the Parc de Bruxelles, designed by Guimard in c1775 and once the royal hunting grounds. On the east side is the Église de St.-Jacques-sur-Coudenberg.

Museums The palace of Charles de Lorraine (1766) is a lovely neoclassical building just off the square, under which sits the Museum of Modern Art (▷ 29). You can visit the northern wing of the palace to see objects that reveal Charles's interest in the Enlightenment. The Hôtel Bellevue, near the Palais Royal, is now the fascinating BELvue Museum (▷ 35), focusing on Belgian history, which also gives access to the remains of the 11th-century Coudenberg Palace. Victor Horta's Palais des Beaux Arts (1928) is now a lively arts space (BOZAR, ▷ 35) with a Film Museum next door.

Palais Royal On the nearby place de Palais is the Palais Royal, the King's offical residence, although in the last decades the royals have lived in their Laeken palace (▷ 102). The Palais de la Nation, on rue de la Loi, is now the Belgian Parliament.

THE BASICS

🞤 E6
🚇 Trône/Gare Centrale/Centraal Station
🚋 Tram 92, 93, 94
Église de St.-Jacques-sur-Coudenberg
🕐 Daily 10–5.45; services Sun 9.45am in English
🚫 None 🎫 Free
Palais Royal
🕐 31 Jul–10 Sep, Tue–Sun 10.30–4.30
♿ Good 🎫 Free

HIGHLIGHTS

● Old and Modern Art Museums (▷ 29–31)
● Palace of Charles de Lorraine
● A stroll in the Parc de Bruxelles, with its tree-lined avenue and fountain

---

DID YOU KNOW?

● The one-day Mont des Arts Pass (€11), available on weekends, gives access to all the museums around the place Royale, as well as concerts and kids' activities.

Le Sablon

Browsing the weekend antiques market at Le Sablon

THE BASICS

➕ E6
☎ Church: 02 511 5741
🕐 Church: Mon–Sat 9–7
🍴 Restaurants, cafés
🚌 20, 48; tram 91, 92, 93, 94
♿ Good
🔗 Les Marolles (▷ 36), art museums (▷ 29–31), place Royale (▷ 33), Musée des Instruments de Musique (▷ 32)
❓ Antiques market Sat 9–6, Sun 9–2

HIGHLIGHTS

● Église de Notre Dame du Sablon
● Statues on the place du Petit Sablon
● Antiques market and shops
● Garden behind Palais d'Egmont
● Patisserie Wittamer (▷ 41)
● Pierre Marcolini chocolates (▷ 41)

The Sablon district, with its Grand and Petit Sablon squares, is the focus of the antiques trade. It is also perfect for strolling, and its terraces are lovely places to sit and watch the world go by.

La place du Grand Sablon Many of Brussels' 17th-century aristocracy and bourgeoisie lived in this elegant square, which is now popular with antiques traders. The square has many specialist food shops, including Patisserie Wittamer (▷ 41), selling wonderful cakes, and Pierre Marcolini (▷ 41), with amazing chocolates.

La place du Petit Sablon Mayor Charles Buls commissioned this square in 1890. The statue of the Counts of Egmont and Horne, who were beheaded by the Duke of Alba because of their religion, was moved here from the Grand' Place and is surrounded by statues of 16th-century scholars and humanists. Behind the garden, the 16th-century Palais d'Egmont, rebuilt in the early 20th century after a fire, is used for receptions by the Ministry of Foreign Affairs.

Église de Notre Dame du Sablon The 15th-century church of Notre Dame du Sablon is a fine example of flamboyant Gothic architecture, built over an earlier chapel with a miraculous statue of the Virgin Mary. A hemp weaver from Antwerp heard celestial voices telling her to steal the Madonna statue at the church where she worshipped and take it to Brussels. The choir and stained-glass windows are particularly beautiful.

More to See

BELVUE MUSEUM

www.belvue.be

This interesting museum reveals the history of Belgium since independence in 1830. It is housed in the Hôtel Bellevue, built in the late 18th century on the ruins of the 11th-century castle of the Dukes of Brabant, later Emperor Charles V's Coudenberg Palace. The museum gives access to the archaeological site of these impressive ruins.

➕ E–F6 ✉ 7 place des Palais ☎ 02 545 0800 🕐 Jun–end Sep Tue–Sun 10–6; Oct–end May Tue–Sun 10–5 🚇 Parc/Park 🚶 Good 🎟 Inexpensive 🍴 Excellent

BOURSE

The Belgian Stock Exchange is in an elegant 1873 building with a frieze by Albert-Ernest Carrier-Belleuse and sculptures by Auguste Rodin. Under the Bourse is the archaeological site of Bruxellae 1238—the ruins of a 13th-century Franciscan convent. You can visit on the first Wednesday of every month at 11.15am and 3pm.

➕ D5 ✉ 2 rue H. Maus ☎ 02 509 1211 🕐 Mon–Fri for groups by prior arrangement

🚇 Bourse/Beurs 🚋 Tram 23, 52, 55, 56, 81 🚶 Few 🎟 Inexpensive

BOZAR

www.bozar.be

The BOZAR, formerly the Palais des Beaux Arts, was designed by Victor Horta in 1928. He left the flamboyant art nouveau style of his earlier buildings behind and opted for a sterner Modernist construction. This is a lively venue for concerts and exhibitions of modern and contemporary art. It also houses the Musée du Cinema.

➕ E5–6 ✉ 23 rue Ravenstein ☎ 02 507 8200 🚇 Parc/Park 🚶 Good 🎟 Varies

CATHÉDRALE ST.-MICHEL ET STE.-GUDULE

www.cathedralestmichel.be

With its intriguing mixture of styles and influences, the cathedral of St.-Michel and Ste.-Gudule expresses Brussels' ability to compromise and is a fitting venue for state occasions. The earlier Romano-Gothic elements, particularly the ambulatory and choir, fit happily with those from the Late Gothic

A 16th-century stained-glass window and the striking façade of the Cathédrale St.-Michel et Ste.-Gudule

period, which are in the nave and on the west façade. Restoration work since 1983 has exposed elements of an earlier church (founded 1047) on which the cathedral was built.

🔆 E5 ⊠ parvis St.-Gudule ☎ 02 217 8345 ⏱ Daily 8–6 🚇 Gare Centrale/ Centraal Station ♿ Few 🍴 Inexpensive ❓ Services Mon–Fri 7.30am, 8am, 12.30pm; Sat 4pm, 5.30pm; Sun 10am, 11.30am, 12.30pm

LA CENTRALE ÉLECTRIQUE/ DE ELEKTRICITEITSCENTRALE

www.brupass.be

Brussels' first ever power plant, built in 1903, now houses the European Centre for Contemporary Art. The large space hosts avant-garde art and organizes workshops for children.

🔆 D4 ⊠ 44 place Ste.-Catherine ☎ 02 279 6444 ⏱ Wed–Sun 11–6, Thu 11–8 🍴 Moderate

ÉGLISE ST.-NICOLAS

The oldest church in Brussels was founded in the 11th century, but most of the interior dates from the 18th. The curved building once followed the line of the River Senne, and a cannonball in the wall recalls the city's bombardment of 1695.

🔆 E5 ⊠ 1 rue au Beurre ☎ 02 513 8022 ⏱ Closed for restoration; due to reopen some time in 2007 🚇 Bourse/Beurs 🚋 Tram 23, 52, 55, 56, 81 🍴 Free

LES MAROLLES

Dwarfed by the Palais de Justice and hemmed in by the elegant Sablon quarter, the Marolles is a reminder of working-class Brussels, with its narrow cobbled streets and junk shops. It stretches roughly from the Porte de Hal to the Église Notre-Dame-de-la-Chapelle; rue Blaes and rue Haute are its main thoroughfares. Around place du Jeu de Balle are traditional cafés and junk shops. The junk market held here has unusual objects at bargain prices, especially on Sunday mornings, the market's liveliest time. A fashionable crowd is slowly moving into the Marolles, and in recent years several art galleries, trendy cafés and nightclubs have opened their doors.

🔆 D7 ⊠ Around place du Jeu de Balle

You'll find no shortage of interesting and unusual items in the flea market at Les Marolles

Porte de Hal/Hallepoort 🚌 20, 48; tram 91 ⛺ Few ❓ Junk market daily 7am–2pm

MUSÉE DE LA VILLE DE BRUXELLES

www.brucity.be

This 19th-century building, a careful reconstruction of the original Maison du Roi, is devoted to Brussels' history, and displays paintings, tapestries, maps and manuscripts, as well as the wardrobe of Manneken Pis (▷ 28).
✚ E5 ✉ Grand' Place ☎ 02 279 4350 🕐 Tue–Sun 10–5 🚇 Bourse/Beurs, Gare Centrale/Centraal Station ⛺ Few 💷 Inexpensive

PALAIS DE JUSTICE

The Palais de Justice was one of Leopold II's pet projects, designed by Poelaert in grand eclectic style. The interior is as overwhelming as the views over Brussels from the terrace. It still contains the main law courts.
✚ D–E7 ✉ place Poelaert ☎ 02 508 6410 🕐 Mon–Fri 9–3. Closed holidays 🚇 Louise/Louiza 🚌 Tram 92, 93, 94 ⛺ Very good 💷 Free

ST.-GÉRY AND STE.-CATHERINE

Brussels was founded on the place St.-Géry in 979, when Charles, Duke of Lorraine, built a castle here. Now the square is a happening place, with many bars. Rue Antoine Dansaert has stylish shops and rue des Chartreuses and chaussée de Flandres have great bars and restaurants. For good fish restaurants, try place Ste.-Catherine.
✚ D4–5 ✉ Around the rue Antoine Dansaert and place St.-Géry 🚇 Bourse/Beurs, Ste.-Catherine/St.-Katelijne ⛺ Good

THÉÂTRE ROYAL DE LA MONNAIE

www.lamonnaie.be

This 1697 theatre was enlarged in 1819 by Napoleon to become one of the most beautiful in the world. It was here the Belgian Revolution began in August 1830. In 1985 the theatre was again enlarged, with a ceiling by Sam Francis and tiling by Sol Lewitt. The opera performances are outstanding.
✚ E4–5 ✉ place de la Monnaie ☎ 02 229 1200 🚇 De Brouckère ⛺ Very good ❓ Tours available

Relaxing in a bar in St.-Géry

From Manneken to Jeanneke Pis

This walk explores the historical heart of Brussels, with the Grand' Place and the now-trendy area of St.-Géry, where the city was born.

DISTANCE: 1.5km (1 mile)   **ALLOW:** 1–2 hours

START

GRAND' PLACE ▷ 26–27
🔲 E5 🚇 Gare Centrale or Bourse

END

RUE DES BOUCHERS
🔲 E5 🚇 Gare Centrale or Bourse

1 Leave the Grand' Place (▷ 26; pictured right) via rue Charles Buls. Walk along rue de l'Etuve, leading to Manneken Pis (▷ 28).

2 Turn right onto rue Grands-Carmes to the rue Marché du Charbon. Walk past Église Notre-Dame du Bon-Secours to boulevard Anspach.

3 Turn right onto the boulevard and then left onto rue des Riches Claires, with a 17th-century church. Turn right onto rue de la Grand Île.

4 Immediately left, a passageway leads to the back of the church and the original site of the River Senne. Return to place St.-Géry.

8 Take a right onto rue des Fripiers and left onto rue Grétry, which becomes rue des Bouchers, where Jeanneke-Pis is signposted.

7 This leads to place Ste.-Catherine, built on the basin of Brussels' old port. Walk past the Tour Noire, part of the first city wall, back to boulevard Anspach, and cross over rue de l'Evêque to place de la Monnaie, with the Théâtre Royal de la Monnaie.

6 Walk along rue du Pont de la Carpe and then left onto rue Antoine Dansaert, where there are restaurants and clothes shops. Take a right onto rue du Vieux Marché aux Grains.

5 A plaque on a covered market shows the site of Brussels' origins.

WALK

CENTRAL BRUSSELS

Shopping

A. M. SWEET
Tea salon and shop with beautiful chocolates, crystallized flowers, *pain d'épices* and coffees.

🔢 D5 ✉ 4 rue des Chartreux
☎ 02 513 5131 🕐 Tue–Sat 9–6.30 🚇 Bourse/Beurs

ANTICYCLONE DES AÇORES
www.anticyclonedesacores.com
A great travel bookshop with travel guides, maps, globes and travel litera-ture in several languages.

🔢 D4 ✉ 34 rue Fossé aux Loups ☎ 02 217 5246
🕐 Mon–Sat 10.30–6.30 🚇 De Brouckère

ANTIK BLAES
Two floors of funky, European home and shop furniture (mostly 1940s–1980s), and a few intriguing curiosities.

🔢 D6 ✉ 51–53 rue Blaes
☎ 02 512 1299 🕐 Daily 10–6
🚊 20, 21, 48

AU GRAND RASOIR (MAISON JAMART)
A beautiful knife shop, supplier to the royal family, with an incredible selection. Repairs, sharpening, re-silvering.

🔢 E5 ✉ 7 rue de l'Hôpital (place St.-Jean) ☎ 02 512 4962 🕐 Mon–Sat 9.30–6.30
🚇 Gare Centrale/Centraal Station 🚊 34, 48, 95, 96

AU SUISSE
The traditional deli to buy smoked fish, cheeses, charcuterie (cold cuts) and other delicacies. Try the house special,

filet Américain, a steak tartare. The sandwich bar next door of the same name is also a Brussels institution.

🔢 D5 ✉ 73–75 boulevard Anspach ☎ 02 512 9589
🕐 Mon, Wed–Fri 10–8, Tue 10–7.30, Sat 10–9, Sun 5–9
🚇 Bourse/Beurs 🚊 Tram 23, 52, 55, 56, 81

LE BONHEUR-EPICERIE AUDIOVISUELLE
www.lebonheur.net
This tiny store has a huge collection of mostly experimental music, videos and DVDs, and a good selection of art-house movies.

🔢 E5 ✉ 53 rue des Eperonniers ☎ 02 511 6414;
🕐 Mon–Sat 11–7, Sun 2–7
🚇 Gare Centrale

LA BOUTIQUE DE TINTIN
www.tintin.be
Tintin fans come here for everything from pyjamas, socks, cups and diaries to life-size statues of Tintin and his friend Abdullah and, of course, the books.

🔢 D5 ✉ 13 rue de la Colline
☎ 02 514 5152 🕐 Mon–Sat 10–6, Sun 11–5 🚇 Gare Centrale/Centraal Station

STAMPS
Brussels is an important hub for stamp collectors. There are many stamp shops cater-ing for all levels, and most are on or around the rue du Midi, near the Bourse.

BRÜSEL
www.brusel.com
Large bookstore selling famous comic strips, mainly in French but also in English, Dutch, German and Spanish.

🔢 D5 ✉ 100 boulevard Anspach ☎ 02 511 0809
🕐 Mon–Sat 10.30–6.30
🚇 Bourse/Beurs 🚊 Tram 23, 52, 55, 56, 81

CHRISTA RENIERS
www.christareniers.com
Beautiful contemporary jewellery with a touch of Zen and no shortage of wit. Reniers' silver cufflinks and keyrings are fun, and the bracelets, rings and earrings have an elegance of their own.

🔢 D5 ✉ 29 rue Antoine Dansaert ☎ 02 510 0660
🕐 Mon–Sat 10.30–1, 2–6.30
🚇 Bourse/Beurs

CHRISTOPHE COPPENS
Renowned Belgian hat maker, who makes hats in all sorts of materials, from the most traditional and classic to the outra-geous and wacky. Most are for women but there are also some for men.

🔢 D4 ✉ 2 rue Léon Lepage
☎ 02 512 7797 🕐 Tue–Sat 11–6 🚇 Ste.-Catherine

DANDOY
This beautiful bakery, founded in 1829, sells Brussels cookies such as *pain à la Grecque*, *speculoos* and *coucque de Dinant* in all sizes and shapes, as well as

Belgium's best marzipan. Once you are inside, this place is hard to resist!
🔢 E5 ✉ 31 rue au Beurre (other branch at 14 rue Charles Buls) ☎ 02 511 8179
🕐 Mon–Sat 8.30–6.30, Sun 10–6.30 🚇 Bourse/Beurs
🚊 Tram 23, 52, 55, 56, 81

ESPACE BIZARRE
www.espacebizzare.com
Large store selling everything for modern living, from Japanese beds and Scandinavian furniture to candles and tableware.
🔢 D5 ✉ 17–19b rue des Chartreux ☎ 02 514 5256
🕐 Mon–Sat 10–7
🚇 Bourse/Beurs

FNAC
www.fnac.be
Brussel's largest bookshop, with titles in French, Dutch, English, German, Italian and Spanish, and a good music department.
🔢 E4 ✉ City 2, rue Neuve ☎ 02 275 1111 🕐 Mon–Thu, Sat 10–7, Fri 10–8 🚇 Rogier or De Brouckère 🚊 Tram 23, 52, 55, 56, 81

GODIVA
The most famous chocolatier of all, with shops around the world.
🔢 E5 ✉ 22 Grand' Place ☎ 02 511 2537 🕐 Mon–Sat 9am–midnight, Sun 10am–midnight 🚇 Gare Centrale/Centraal Station

K. GRUSENMEYER
www.grusenmeyer.be
Wonderful antiques shop specializing in tribal and oriental sculpture

and objects d'art, and exquisite 18th- and 19th-century Chinese furniture.
🔢 E6 ✉ rue Lebeau 14 ☎ 02 514 03 37 🕐 Mon–Sat 11–6 🚇 Porte de Namur 🚊 Tram 91, 92, 93, 94

MARTIN MARGIELA
Flagship store of the cult Belgian designer.
🔢 D4 ✉ 40 rue Léon Lepage ☎ 02 223 7520
🕐 Mon–Sat 11–7 🚇 Bourse/Beurs, Ste.-Catherine

MARY'S
This traditional shop, specializing in homemade pralines and *marrons glacés*, is well known among chocolate lovers.
🔢 F4 ✉ 73 rue Royale ☎ 02 217 4500 🕐 Mon–Sat 9.30–6 🚇 Botanique/Kruidtuin 🚊 Tram 92, 93, 94

PATISSERIE WITTAMER
www.wittamer.com
This wonderful but expensive patisserie sells Brussels' best sorbets, excellent chocolates and cakes that taste as good as they look.
🔢 E6 ✉ 6 place du Grand

GALERIES ST.-HUBERT
This elegant covered arcade has new and traditional stores. It was built in 1846–47, when this type of shopping mall was a first in Europe.
✉ Rue du Marché-aux-Herbes 🚇 Gare Centrale/Centraal Station ♿ Good

Sablon ☎ 02 512 3742 🕐 Mon 9–6, Tue–Sat 7–7, Sun 7–6 🚊 Tram 92, 93, 94

PIERRE MARCOLINI
www.marcolini.be
Marcolini is winner of the Chocolatier of the World award, and his chocolate creations are some of the best, and most expensive, in Belgium. (Also at 75 avenue Louise and 1302 chaussée de Waterloo.)
🔢 E6 ✉ 1 rue des Minimes ☎ 02 514 1206 🕐 Tue–Sun 10–6 🚊 34, 48, 95, 96; tram 92, 93, 94

PLAIZIER
www.plaizier.be
A beautiful shop with an excellent selection of photographic postcards, posters, books and other visually pleasing objects.
🔢 E5 ✉ 50 rue des Eperonniers ☎ 02 513 4730
🕐 Mon–Sat 11–6 🚇 Gare Centrale/Centraal Station

STIJL
In her temple of Belgian fashion Sonja Noël stocks the best established designers like Dries Van Noten and Anne Demeulemeester, and promotes new designers. Down the road at No. 34 is Kat en Muis, her shop for fashionable kids, and at No. 47 Stijl Underwear.
🔢 D4 ✉ 74 rue Antoine Dansaert ☎ 02 512 0313
🕐 Mon–Sat 10.30–6.30
🚇 Bourse/ Beurs, Ste.-Catherine/St.-Katelijne
🚊 63; tram 23, 52, 55, 56, 81

Entertainment and Nightlife

ACTORS STUDIO
Two-screen repertory cinema showing five films a day, mainly 'B' movies and good films from non-European countries.
🔢 E5 ✉ 16 petite rue des Bouchers ☎ 02 512 1696 🚇 De Brouckère

A LA MORT SUBITE
www.alamortsubite.be
This traditional bar was one of singer Jacques Brel's preferred watering holes. It even has its own brew, called Mort Subite (Sudden Death) because of its higher alcohol content.
🔢 E5 ✉ 7 rue Montagne aux Herbes Potagères ☎ 02 513 1318 🕐 Daily 11am–midnight 🚇 Gare Centrale/Centraal station

ANCIENNE BELGIQUE
www.abconcerts.be
One of Brussels' best rock venues, revamped as a showcase for the Flemish community.
🔢 D5 ✉ 110 boulevard Anspach ☎ 02 548 2424 🚇 Bourse/Beurs

L'ARCHIDUC
Funky, smoky art deco lounge designed like a cruise ship. It plays jazz or 1930s music.
🔢 D5 ✉ 6 rue A. Dansaert, ☎ 02 512 0652 🕐 Daily 4pm–6am 🚇 Bourse/Beurs

ARENBERG GALERIES
www.arenberg.be
This tiny but delightful cinema, in a converted art deco theatre in the Galeries St.-Hubert, specializes in repertory cinema and foreign films, including movies from Asia and the Middle East.
🔢 E5 ✉ 26 galerie de la Reine ☎ 02 512 8063 🚇 Gare Centrale/Centraal Station

AU SOLEIL
Popular bar in a former traditional men's clothing shop. There are tables outside in summer.
🔢 D5 ✉ 86 rue du Marché au Charbon ☎ 02 513 3430 🕐 Daily 10am–1am (Fri, Sat until 2am) 🚇 Bourse/Beurs 🚊 Tram 23, 52, 55, 56, 81, 90

LE BAZAAR
A hot-air balloon hovers over the bar, and hundreds of candles make it perfect for a romantic dinner on the ground floor, but better to hit the dance floor in the basement, where funk, soul and disco music rule.
🔢 D7 ✉ 63 rue des Capucins ☎ 02 511 2600 🕐 Thu–Sat 7.30pm–4am 🚇 Porte de Hal/ Halleepoort

TICKETS
Tickets for most big events in Brussels can be booked (at a small charge) through the tourist office on the Grand' Place (☎ 02 513 8940; www.bitc.be); Auditorium 44 (☎ 02 218 2735) on boulevard du Jardin Botanique 44; or FNAC in City 2, rue Neuve (☎ 02 275 1111).

BEURSSCHOUWBURG
www.beursschouwburg.be
The 19th-century theatre of the Stock Exchange is now a venue for rock concerts, jazz, North African rai and avant-garde Belgian theatre.
🔢 D5 ✉ 22 rue Auguste Orts ☎ 02 550 0350 🚇 Bourse/Beurs 🚊 Tram 23, 52, 55, 56, 81

LE BOTANIQUE
www.botanique.be
The botanical gardens are now a cultural venue for the French-speaking community. See rock concerts in the Orangerie and world music events like the *Festival de la Chanson* in September.
🔢 F4 ✉ 236 rue Royale ☎ 02 226 1211 🚇 Botanique 🚊 38, 61; tram 92, 94

CAFÉ CENTRAL
www.lecafecentral.com
Small but great venue, with a dance floor in the back and a cinema. Concerts twice a month (usually Thursday 10pm).
🔢 D5 ✉ 14 rue de Borgval ☎ 0486 722624 🚇 Bourse/Beurs

CONSERVATOIRE ROYAL DE MUSIQUE
www.conservatoire.be
Another perfect venue for chamber orchestras, partly designed by the famous organ builder Cavaillé-Coll.
🔢 E6 ✉ 30 rue de la Régence ☎ 02 511 0427; 🚇 Gare Centrale/Centraal Station or Louise

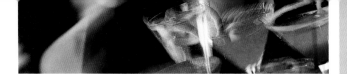

THE FUSE
www.fuse.be
Brussels' premier techno club has DJs from the US, London and Amsterdam. Gay night is on Sunday.
🔲 D6 ✉ 208 rue Blaes ☎ 02 511 9789 🕐 From 10pm 🚇 Porte de Hal/Hallepoort 🚊 27, 48

HALLES DE SCHAERBEEK
www.halles.be
This superb 19th-century covered market is now a major cultural venue for the French-speaking community, with regular music, dance and drama.
🔲 G3 ✉ 22b rue Royal Ste.-Marie, Schaerbeek ☎ 02 218 2107 🚇 Botanique/Botaniek

KAAITHEATER
www.kaaitheater.be
A jewel of 1930s architecture, this former cinema houses the Flemish Theatre Institute. There are performances by influential Belgian dancers.
🔲 D3 ✉ 20 square Sainctelette ☎ Box office 02 201 5959 🚇 Yser/Ijzer

MIRANO DIRTY DANCING
www.mirano.be
Fashionable crowds of thirtysomethings frequent this former cinema, where house music is king. Dress up or they might not let you in.
🔲 G4 ✉ 38 chaussée de Louvain ☎ 02 227 3948 🕐 Fri, Sat 10pm–6am 🚇 Madou

MUSÉE DU CINÉMA
www.cinematheque.be
Besides the permanent exhibition, five films are shown daily. Two are silent films accompanied by piano music. This is the place to see the old cinema classics, as well as more recent movies and little-known jewels from around the world.
🔲 E5–6 ✉ Palais des Beaux-Arts, 9 rue Baron Horta ☎ 02 507 8370 🕐 Daily 5.30–10.30 🚇 Gare Centrale/Centraal Station 🚊 Tram 92, 93, 94

MUSIC VILLAGE
www.themusicvillage.com
Lively jazz café with jazz concerts, from the traditional to the most experimental, as well as world music such as flamenco.
🔲 D5 ✉ 50 rue des Pierres ☎ 02 513 1345 🕐 Dinner from 7pm, concerts from 9pm 🚇 De Brouckère, Bourse

PALAIS DES BEAUX ARTS (BOZAR)
www.bozar.be
This art nouveau complex is Brussels' most prestigious concert venue. Its two halls, with perfect acoustics, are home to the Philharmonic Society and the Orchestre National de Belgique. Most of the city's big concerts take place here.
🔲 E5–6 ✉ 23 rue Ravenstein ☎ Box office: 02 507 8200; 24-hour information 02 507 8444 🕐 Box office: Mon–Sat 9–7 🚇 Parc/Park or Gare Centrale/Centraal Station

RECYCLART
www.recyclart.be
The old train station is divided into several spaces where concerts, puppet performances and other more alternative happenings are held.
🔲 D6 ✉ Station Bruxelles-Chapelle, 25 rue des Ursulines ☎ 02 502 5734 🚇 Gare Centrale/Anneesens

THÉÂTRE NATIONAL
www.theatrenational.be
The National Theatre often arranges co-productions with Strasbourg. Most plays are in French, with a few English-speaking touring companies.
🔲 D5 ✉ 85 boulevard Anspach ☎ 02 203 5303 🕐 Box office Mon–Sat 11–6 🚇 Bourse/Beurs

THÉÂTRE ROYAL DE LA MONNAIE
See page 37.

Restaurants

PRICES

Prices are approximate, based on a 3-course meal for one person.

€€€	over €45
€€	€20–€45
€	under €20

BELGAQUEEN (€€)

www.resto.be/belgaqueen
An excellent brasserie, the Belaqueen has it all—a wonderful oyster bar with an almost endless choice, a beer bar and a cigar bar, all set in a lofty building with a huge stained-glass skylight. As the name says, everything is very Belgian, from the architecture to the refined contemporary food; beer is used in many dishes.

➕ D4 ✉ 32 rue Fossé aux Loups ☎ 02 217 2187
🕐 Daily 12–2.30, 7–midnight
🚇 De Brouckère 🚋 Tram 23, 52, 55, 56, 81

LA BELLE MARAÎCHÈRE (€€–€€€)

A well-known traditional fish restaurant on Brussels' old port. The waterzooi (fish stew) is excellent and set menus are great value.

➕ D4 ✉ 11 place Ste.-Catherine ☎ 02 512 9759
🕐 Fri–Tue lunch, dinner
🚇 Ste.-Catherine/St.-Katelijne
🚋 Tram 23, 52, 55, 56, 81, 90

BOCCONI (€€€)

www.ristorantebocconi.com
At the best Italian restaurant in town you'll find stylish décor, excellent and innovative Italian dishes and attentive but relaxed service.

➕ E5 ✉ Hotel Amigo, rue de l'Amigo 1 ☎ 02 547 4715
🕐 Lunch, dinner 🚇 Gare Centrale/Centrall station, Bourse/Beurs

BONSOIR CLARA (€€–€€€)

www.bonsoirclara.be
This trendy and busy brasserie-style eaterie is in a fashionable street, with a vibrant setting. Come here to enjoy excellent Mediterranean food.

➕ D5 ✉ 22 rue Antoine Dansaert ☎ 02 502 0990
🕐 Mon–Fri lunch, dinner; Sat dinner 🚇 Bourse/Beurs

RUE DES BOUCHERS

Many Bruxellois try to avoid the rue des Bouchers (Butchers' Street), near the Grand' Place, where at some of the restaurants racoleurs (hustlers) harass the passing tourists to enter their establishment. In the 1950s it was a seedy area of cabarets and cafés that doubled up as brothels. At No. 30 Petite Rue des Bouchers was the cabaret La Rose Noire, where famous Belgian singers such as Jacques Brel made their first appearances. The cabaret was demolished in 1964; the last café, Le Bourgeoys, closed in 2001.

LE CERCLE DES VOYAGEURS (€€)

www.lecercledesvoyageurs.com
Grand café with leather armchairs and a colonial atmosphere where visitors feel at home. The menu includes dishes from around the world and the wine list is also global.

➕ D5 ✉ 18 rue des Grands Carmes ☎ 02 514 3949
🕐 Daily 11am–late
🚇 Anneessens

CLAUDE DUPONT (€€€)

www.resto.be/claudedupont
One of the country's top chefs, Claude Dupont has been cooking at his superb traditional family restaurant for about five years. He offers French-Belgium cuisine of the highest standards. Try one of the set menus that include dishes like goose liver cooked in Muscat wine, monkfish sashimi, river eels and duck.

➕ Off map at A1 ✉ 46 avenue Vital Riethuisenlaan, Ganshoren/Koekelberg
☎ 02 426 0000 🕐 Wed–Sun lunch, dinner; closed 2 Jul–7 Aug 🚇 Basilique

COMOCOMO (€€)

www.comocomo.com
A Basque pintxo (tapas) bar is quite something, but this restaurant takes it one step farther and has the dishes going around on a sushi conveyor belt. The style is ultra contemporary and the food,

including wild boar carpaccio, fried garlicky mushrooms and quails legs, is really good.
🔒 D5 ✉ 19 rue Antoine Dansaert ☎ 02 503 0303
🕐 Daily 12–3, 7–11
🚇 Bourse/Beurs

COMME CHEZ SOI (€€€)
www.commechezsoi.be
By common consent, this is Belgium's finest restaurant (quite something in a country with so many fine restaurants). Comme Chez Soi has three Michelin stars, as well as very loyal customers to prove it. You need to reserve weeks ahead as there are only 40 seats.
🔒 D6 ✉ 23 place Rouppe
☎ 02 512 2921
🕐 Tue–Sat 12–1.30, 7–9.30. Closed Jul 🚇 Anneessens

DARINGMAN (€)
Old-fashioned brown café turned trendy, where the old locals meet the fashionable crowd.
🔒 D5 ✉ 37 rue de Flandre
☎ 02 512 4323
🕐 Tue–Thu noon–1am, Fri noon–2am, Sat 4pm–2am
🚇 Ste.-Catherine/St.-Katelijne

DIVINO (€–€€)
Straightforward but very popular Italian restaurant with huge wood-oven baked pizzas and home-made pastas.
🔒 D5 ✉ 56 rue des Chartreux ☎ 02 503 3909
🕐 Mon–Fri lunch, dinner; Sat, Sun dinner 🚇 Bourse

DOMAINE DE LINTILLAC (€€)
A 1970s-style restaurant with whitewashed walls and wooden beams, red gingham table cloths and lots of candles. The food, dishes from southwest France, is excellent, with the best foie gras in town at the most reasonable prices. Excellent service and warm atmosphere.
🔒 D4 ✉ 25 rue de Flandre
☎ 02 511 5123 🕐 Mon dinner, Tue–Sat lunch, dinner
🚇 Ste.-Catherine/St.-Katelijne

LE FALSTAFF (€–€€)
At some time during an evening out everyone usually ends up at this huge but always busy art deco café with a vast terrace, heated in winter.
🔒 D5 ✉ 19–25 rue Henri

101 RESTAURANTS
Rue Dansaert has its fair share of trendy eateries, as does rue des Chartreux, but Brussels' ultra-hip diners now head for the nearby chaussée de Flandres/Vlaamsche Steenweg. This street is packed with eating possibilities, from the very Belgian and excellent Viva M'Boma (▷ 46) and Le Pré Salé at No. 18, to rustic French with lots of foie gras at Le Domaine de Lintillac (▷ above). Henri at No. 113–115 is a simple but hip restaurant with fusion cuisine or you can have tea at the bookshop Bollebooks.

Maus ☎ 02 511 8789
🕐 Daily 10am–2am
🚇 Bourse/Beurs 🚊 Tram 23, 52, 55, 56, 81, 90

KASBAH, RESTAURANT AND SALON (€€)
In a delightful dark-blue cave setting, this popular Moroccan restaurant delivers with its large menu of tajines, couscous and grills accompanied by Arabic music. Try the excellent Sunday brunch.
🔒 D5 ✉ 20 rue Antoine Dansaert ☎ 02 502 4026
🕐 Mon–Fri lunch, dinner; Sat, Sun dinner 🚇 Bourse/Beurs
🚊 Tram 23, 52, 55, 56, 81

LITTLE ASIA (€€)
Popular, contemporary restaurant with excellent Vietnamese dishes, as well as Thai and Chinese dishes. Attentive service.
🔒 D4 ✉ 8 rue Ste.-Catherine
☎ 02 502 8836 🕐 Mon–Sat 12–11 🚇 Bourse/Beurs
🚊 Tram 23, 52, 55, 56, 81

LA MANUFACTURE (€€)
www.lamanufacture.be
This restaurant, in the old Delvaux leather factory, serves delicious, inventive European food with a touch of Asia. You can sit outside in summer.
🔒 C–D5 ✉ 12 rue Notre-Dame du Sommeil
☎ 02 502 2525 🕐 Mon–Fri lunch, dinner; Sat dinner
🚇 Bourse/Beurs 🚊 Tram 23, 52, 55, 56, 81, 90

LE PAIN QUOTIDIEN/ HET DAGELYJKS BROOD (€)

In this chain of tea rooms, breakfast, lunch, snacks and afternoon tea are served around one big table. Try the breads, croissants, pastries and jams—they are all home-made.

🚇 E6 ✉ 11 rue des Sablons ☎ 02 513 5154 🕐 7.30–7 🚌 4, 95; tram 20, 48; 🚇 D5 ✉ 16 Rue Antoine Dansaert ☎ 02 502 2361 🕐 7.30–7

RESOURCE (€€)

If you share the views of the Slow Food movement, try this well-kept secret with superb food at very reasonable prices. This is a place to stay a while as the menu includes several courses, each more pleasurable than the other.

🚇 D6 ✉ 164 rue du Midi ☎ 02 514 3223 🕐 Tue–Sat 12–2.30, 7–10 🚇 Anneessens

SAHBAZ (€–€€)

Slightly away from the heart of town, but this Turkish restaurant is one of the best in Brussels, and worth the small excursion. Turkish and *Bruxellois* families come here for the hearty and inexpensive kebabs, stews and delicious Turkish pizzas.

🚇 G3 ✉ 102 chaussée de Haecht ☎ 02 217 0277 🕐 Thu–Tue 11.30–3, 6–midnight 🚌 Tram 92, 93

TAVERNE DU PASSAGE (€–€€)

This elegant brasserie (founded 1928) is known for its *croquettes au crevettes* (shrimp croquettes) and traditional Brussels cuisine. The *choucroute au jambon* (saurerkraut with ham) is a must.

🚇 D5 ✉ 30 Galerie de la Reine ☎ 02 512 3732 🕐 Daily 12–12 🚇 Gare Centrale/Centraal Station

DE ULTIEME HALLUCINATIE (€€)

Worth a visit just for the splendid art nouveau interior, but the French food also lives up to expectation. The goose- and duck-liver dishes are delicious, as is the poached fish in gueuze sauce.

🚇 F4 ✉ 316 rue Royale ☎ 02 217 0614 🕐 Mon–Fri lunch, dinner; Sat 5pm–3am 🚇 Botanique/Kruidtuin

---

STREET OF THE WORLD

The rue Antoine Dansaert, in Brussels, has a wide variety of ethnic restaurants in different price ranges. Young *Bruxellois* often choose the inexpensive Vietnamese Da Kao at No. 38 for a quick bite to eat, while the trendy crowd heads for the contemporary Mediterranean cuisine of Bonsoir Clara (▷ 44) and tapas at ComoComo (▷ 44). Next door is the Moroccan Kasbah restaurant.

VINCENT (€€)

www.restaurantvincent.com
A real monument of Brussels cuisine, this is one of the most reliable restaurants in the area. Hunks of meat hang in the window. Inside, the dining room has hand-painted tiles and lots of character. Efficient waiters expertly prepare dishes like steak flambée or steak tartare while you watch.

🚇 E5 ✉ 8/10 rue des Dominicains, off rue des Bouchers ☎ 02 511 2303 🕐 Daily 12–2.45, 6.30–11.30 🚇 De Brouckère/Gare Centrale/Centraal Station

VISMET (€€€)

Superb fish restaurant with an open kitchen, a plain wood and white-tablecloth décor but delicious fish and seafood.

🚇 D4 ✉ 23 place Ste.-Catherine ☎ 02 218 8545 🕐 12–2.30, 7–11 🚇 Ste.-Catherine/St.-Katelijne

VIVA M'BOMA (€€€)

'Long Live My Grandma' is an absolutely delightful restaurant in an old butcher's shop, with already several awards in its pocket. It is a modest place, but the food is consistently excellent. The menu has many Belgian dishes, focusing on meat and offal.

🚇 D4 ✉ 17 rue de Flandre ☎ 02 512 15 93 🕐 Wed–Sat lunch, dinner, Mon–Tue lunch 🚇 Ste.-Catherine/ St.-Katelijne

South of the ring road is a newer Brussels, with the more residential areas of Ixelles and St.-Gilles. In recent years these districts have undergone a revival, with a wealth of new shops and restaurants.

Arts-Loi
Kunst-Wet
Rue Stevin
WETSTRAAT
Maelbeek
RUE Maalbeek
DE
Square
Frère-
Orban
Saint
Joseph
BELLIARDSTRAAT
Berlaymont E U
U E Berlaimont
SCHUMAN
Saint
Sacrement
Schuman
Conseil Européen
Europese Rad
Quartier Européen
Europese Wijk
Grande
Mosquée
Pavillon
Horta
Ecole
Militaire
School
Dominicains
Musée Royal d'l'Armée
et d'Hist Militaire
Kon Museum v h Legeren
v d Krijgsgeschiedenis
Le Cinquantenaire
Autoworld
Jubelpark
AVENUE J F KENNEDY LAAN
Trône
Troon
Parlement Européen
(Europees Parlement)
Parc Léopold
Léopoldspark
LUXEMBOURG
LUXEMBURG
Musée
d'Hist Nat
Musée des Siences
Naturelles
Musée voor Natuur-
wetenschappen
Brydel
Musées Roy d'Art et d'Histoire
Kon Musea v Kunst en Geschied
AVENUE DES NERVIENS
NERVIERSLAAN
Saint
Gertrude
Maison
Cauchie
Peres du
Saint Sacrement
N D Immaculée
O L V Onbevlekt
Mais
Comm
Musée des
Beaux-Arts
d'Ixelles
ELSENE
Musée
Wiertz
ETTERBEEK
AVENUE VAN JACOBSLAAN
Saint
Antoine
Veldstraat
Hôtel
Tassel
Saint
Antoine
Hôpital
d'Etterbeek
Hôtel
Solvay
Maison
de la Radio
Sainte Croix
H Kruis
Hôpital
d'Ixelles
Caserne
M Géruzet
Kazerne
Avenue Louise
(Louizalaan)
Caserne
Gal de Witte
de Haelen
Kazerne
ETTERBEEK
Saint
Andrew
Gendarmerie
Saint Philippe
de Néri
Prêtres du
Sacré-Cœur
IXELLES
Musée
Constantin
Meunier
N D de
la Cambre
Abbaye de la Cambre
Abdij ter Kameren
AV EUGÈNE DE MO
Stade de
l'ULB
Stadion
Institute Médico-
Chirurgical Longchamp
CHURCHILLLAAN
BRUSSEL
ULB
VUB
N D du
Saint Rosaire
Bois de
la Cambre
F   G   H   J

Le Cinquantenaire

HIGHLIGHTS

● Treasure Room at the
Musée d'Art et d'Histoire
● Pavillion Horta
● Views over the city from
the top of the triumphal arch

DID YOU KNOW?

● Maison Cauchie, at 5 rue
des Francs (open first weekend of each month 11–1,
2–6), is the finest example of
art nouveau architecture in
Brussels. Paul Cauchie, who
built the house in 1905, was
a sgraffiti painter and the
façade shows his work.

**Built to celebrate 50 years of Belgian
independence, this park has all you
would imagine in the way of grand
buildings—even its own Arc de Triomphe.
It also has some surprises.**

The most famous city park In 1880, Leopold II
ordered the building of the Palais du
Cinquantenaire, with two huge halls, to hold the
National Exhibition in the park. For the next 25
years, the king dreamed about erecting an Arc
de Triomphe. It was finally built in 1905
by Charles Girault, architect of the Petit Palais in
Paris, with two colonnades added in 1918.

Remarkable monuments Several features here
recall important international fairs. An Arab-inspired
building, which housed a painted panorama of

Clockwise from top left: vintage cars at Autoworld; enjoying the Montgomery fountain, in nearby Avenue de Tervuren; silhouette of the Arc de Triomphe; a shining exhibit at Autoworld; red Ferrari cars line up in front of the Arc de Triomphe; remembering a bygone era at Autoworld

Cairo in an 1897 fair, is now Brussels' Grand Mosque. Pavillion Horta (open Tue–Fri 2.30–3.30) was erected in 1889 on designs by Victor Horta to house the *haut-relief* of the *Human Passions*, by the sculptor Jef Lambeaux.

Grand but dusty museums One of the National Exhibition halls now showcases Autoworld, a prestigious collection of vintage cars from 1886 to the 1970s. The Musée Royal de l'Armée et d'Histoire Militaire incorporates an aviation museum, with planes displayed in a huge hangar, and houses weapons from medieval times to the present. The rich Musée Royal d'Art et d'Histoire, in the south wing of the Palais du Cinquantenaire, has items from ancient civilizations, Belgian archaeological discoveries and important European decorative arts and lace.

THE BASICS

✚ H–J6

✉ Main entrances rue de la Loi and avenue du Chevalier

🚇 Mérode, Schuman

🚌 20, 27, 80; tram 81, 82

Autoworld
www.autoworld.be
☎ 02 736 4165
🕐 10–6 (until 5, Oct–Mar)
🍴 Café
♿ Good 💶 Moderate

Army & Military History Museum
www.klm-mra.be
☎ 02 737 7811
🕐 Tue–Sun 9–12, 1–5
🍴 Café
♿ Poor 💶 Free

Musée Royal d'Art et d'Histoire
www.kmkg-mrah.be
☎ 02 741 7211
🕐 Tue–Fri 9.30–5, Sat, Sun 10–5
🍴 Café
♿ Good 💶 Moderate

Musée de Victor Horta

TOP 25

Many of the grand buildings designed by architect Victor Horta have been destroyed, but here in his house, in the rue Américaine, the flowing lines and the play of light and space clarify his vision.

New Style Victor Horta (1861–1947) built these two houses on the rue Américaine as his home and studio between 1898 and 1901. Now a museum, they illustrate the break he made from traditional town houses, with their large, sombre rooms. Horta's are spacious and airy, full of mirrors, white tiles and stained-glass windows. A light shaft in the middle of the house illuminates a banister so gracious and flowing that you just want to slide down it. The attention to detail in the house is amazing, even down to the last door handle, all designed in fluid art nouveau style.

The ornate wrought-iron staircase (left) and the elegant dining room (below)

Art nouveau in St.-Gilles There are other interesting properties in residential St.-Gilles. Strolling around the area between the rue Defacqz and the prison of St.-Gilles you can admire several examples of art nouveau style, dating from the late 19th to early 20th centuries. Paul Hankar designed the Ciambarlani and Janssens mansions at Nos. 48 and 50 rue Defacqz, and his own house at No. 71. One of the most beautiful art nouveau façades in Brussels, designed by Albert Roosenboom, is 85 rue Faider. At No. 83 rue de Livourne you can see the private house of the architect Octave Van Rysselberghe, who also built the Otlet mansion at No. 48 rue de Livourne. The Hannon mansion, built at No. 1 avenue de la Jonction by Jules Brunfaut, is now a photographer's gallery; look for the impressive fresco by Paul-Albert Baudouin in the staircase.

THE BASICS

www.hortamuseum.be
➕ E9
✉ 25 rue Américaine, St.-Gilles
☎ 02 543 0490
🕐 Tue–Sun 2–5.30
🚇 Horta
🚌 54, 60; tram 91, 92 from place Louise
♿ Few
💶 Moderate
❓ Guidebooks and guided tours are available

More to See

AVENUE LOUISE/IXELLES

Avenue Louise is one of the places where you'll see *Bruxellois* heading for the designer boutiques. The avenue, and the trendy Ixelles district, are where Brussels bureaucrats come to spend their money; they crowd the many smart cafés, spilling onto the streets, and part with hundreds of euros in its stores. It is one of Brussels' main shopping areas, with boutiques, interior designers, showrooms, art galleries, hotels and restaurants.

➕ E–F–G7–10 ✉ avenue Louise
🍴 Restaurants nearby 🚇 Louise/Louiza
🚌 34, 54, 60; tram 91, 92, 93, 94
♿ Good

BOIS DE LA CAMBRE

Once part of the Forest of Soignes, this green area was annexed by the city in 1862 and laid out by landscape artist Keilig. Boating, bicycling, fishing and roller-skating are among the activities on offer here.

➕ G11–G12 ✉ Main entrance on avenue Louise 🕐 Dawn–dusk 🚌 Tram 93, 94
♿ Few 🎫 Free

COLLÉGIALE DES STS.-PIERRE ET GUIDON

The Romanesque crypt dates from the 11th century, but the superb Gothic church, with frescoes, is from the 14th to 16th centuries. The altar is illuminated by light filtering through the lovely stained-glass window above. The rare Celtic tombstone is believed to mark the grave of St. Guidon.

➕ Off A7–8 ✉ place de la Vaillance
☎ 02 523 0220 🕐 Daily 9–12, 2–5; services Mon–Thu 8.45am, Fri 6pm, Sat 4.30pm, Sun 5pm. Closed during services 🚇 St.-Guidon/St.-Guido
♿ Few 🎫 Free

EURO PARLIAMENT

The imposing façade of the European Parliament building, made of slick granite, glass and steel, is nicknamed the Caprice des Dieux (whim of the gods). This is where the European Union's 626 members gather when in Brussels.

➕ G6 ✉ rue Wiertz ☎ 02 284 3457
🕐 Audio-guided visits Mon–Thu 10, 3, Fri 10–2.30 🚇 Schuman 🎫 Free

Striking architecture in the European Parliament district

MARCHÉ DU MIDI

The Marché du Midi is one of Europe's largest markets, with fresh fruit and vegetables, fish, meat, clothes, pictures, household goods, North African music and books.

✚ C7 ✉ Near the Gare du Midi ⏰ Sun 7–1 🚇 Gare du Midi/Zuidstation 🚊 Tram 23, 52, 55, 56, 81, 82, 90 ♿ Few 💷 Free

MUSÉE DES BEAUX-ARTS D'IXELLES

www.musee-ixelles.be

Since the 1800s, Ixelles/Elsene has attracted Belgian intellectuals, artists and writers, so a museum of 19th- and 20th-century Belgian art comes as no surprise. Housed in an old slaughterhouse, the collection includes works by Auguste Rodin, who had a studio in the area. What attracts the crowds are the temporary exhibitions of modern art and architecture.

✚ G8 ✉ 71 rue Jean Volsem ☎ 02 515 64 21 ⏰ Tue–Fri 1–6.30, Sat, Sun 10–5 🚊 38, 54, 59, 60, 71; tram 81, 82 💷 Free (moderate for temporary exhibitions) ♿ Moderate wheelchair access

MUSÉE CONSTANTIN MEUNIER

This museum is dedicated to the life and works of Belgian painter and sculptor Constantin Meunier (1831–1905), with more than 150 of his works displayed in what was once his house and studio. Meunier was disturbed by the hard living conditions of the Belgian working class, and became famous for his paintings and sculptures of suffering workers.

✚ F10 ✉ 59 rue de l'Abbaye ☎ 02 648 4449 ⏰ Tue–Fri 10–12, 1–5; alternate weekends 🚇 Louise 🚊 Tram 93, 94 💷 Free ♿ Difficult

MUSÉE DAVID ET ALICE VAN BUUREN

www.museumvanbuuren.com

This delightful museum is in the van Buuren's elegant art deco house. The interior and the gardens are stunning, and the art collection of the banker and his wife is equally remarkable, including Brueghel and van Gogh.

✚ E12 ✉ 41 avenue Léo Errera ☎ 02 343 4851 ⏰ Wed–Mon 2–5.30 🚊 Tram 90 ♿ Few wheelchair facilities 💷 Moderate

Brussels is the political heart of Europe

Art Nouveau Bicycling Tour

Brussels has a wealth of art nouveau architecture. This tour takes in works by two of the main players, Victor Horta and Paul Hankar.

DISTANCE: 4km (2.5 miles) **ALLOW:** 2 hours

START

HÔTEL SOLVAY, AVENUE LOUISE 224
✛ F8–9 🚇 Louise, then tram 93, 94

END

PLACE LOUISE
✛ E7 🚇 Louise

❶ Start at the fine Hôtel Solvay, built by Victor Horta in 1898. Cycle north-west along the avenue Louise and take the third street to the left, rue Paul E. Janson. Here you'll see Hôtel Tassel at No. 6, which was built by Horta in 1893.

❷ Turn right on rue Faider and then left onto rue Defacqz. No. 48 is a house by Paul Hankar, and No. 51 is his studio. Turn left on rue Simonis to the place du Châtelain, with lots of cafés. Continue on rue du Page to the rue Américaine and take a right to the Musée Horta (▷ 52–53).

❸ Continue along the street and take a left on chaussée de Charleroi. No. 55 is the remarkable art nouveau house Les Hiboux (the Owls) and next door is the superb Hôtel Hannon, built in 1903 and now a photo gallery.

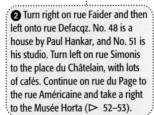

❹ From here take a right on the rue R.F. Delhasse, with two smaller art nouveau houses at Nos. 13–15. Take a right on rue de la Glacière, left on chaussée de Waterloo and immediately right onto avenue Ducpétiaux. Nos. 13, 15 and 47 are houses by Paul Hankar.

❽ Take a right onto rue Jourdan and continue to the place Louise.

❼ Take a left on rue du Métal and then turn right on rue l'Hôtel de Monnaie, with, at No. 66, Hôtel Winssinger, by Horta (1894).

❻ Turn right on rue M. Wilmote and left on rue d'Irlande to the place L. Morichar. Turn right on rue de Roumanie, left on rue de la Croix de St.-Pierre, with (at Nos. 76, 78 and 80) more houses by Paul Hankar.

❺ There are art nouveau houses by lesser-known architects all along the way back. Take a left on rue du Portugal, then right on rue Moris, and left again on rue d'Espagne.

Shopping

ART DECO 1920–1940

After admiring Brussels' amazing art deco and art nouveau façades, you may want to see some period furniture, and that is just what this shop specializes in. Equally impressive is the collection of art deco jewellery.
🞧 D9 ✉ avenue Adolphe Demeur 16, St.-Gilles ☎ 02 534 7025 🕓 Wed–Sat 11–6.30, Sun 11.30–6.30 🚇 Horta

AXL

'Welcome to Ali Baba's Cave!' is how you are greeted in this tiny store. The shop is filled with gorgeous and unusual jewellery and accessories by international designers such as Shaunleane, Wouters & Hendrix and Alexis Bittar. The owners Axelle Delhaye and Meliha Saldo are artists who look for timeless beauty and originality of design, so very often you find new designers or one-off pieces.
🞧 E10 ✉ 16 place Georges Brugmann ☎ 02 346 8957 🕓 Tue–Sat 11–6, Sun 12–3 🚋 Tram 91, 92 from place Louise

BEER MANIA

www.beermania.be
Here you'll find the largest selection of beers in town, with more than 400 types, from the most obvious to some rare and hard-to-find ones. You can also buy the correct glasses for your preferred beer, sample beers in the back of the shop or attend classes or tasting sessions (check the website for English classes).
🞧 F7 ✉ 174–176 chaussée de Wavre ☎ 02 512 1788 🕓 Mon–Sat 10–9 🚇 Porte de Namur/Naamsepoort

CHINE COLLECTION

Designer Luc Duchêne has several Chine collections, always with very wearable, trendy and feminine clothes in beautiful fabrics. A branch is at 2 rue van Artevelde.
🞧 E8 ✉ 82–84 avenue Louise ☎ 02 512 4552 🕓 Mon–Sat 10–6.30 🚇 Louise 🚋 Tram 93, 94

LE DÉPÔT/ LE DÉPÔT JONAS

Le Dépôt is a good place to find the latest comic strips, while le Dépôt Jonas has a vast selection of secondhand comic strips, books, video games and music.
🞧 F7 ✉ 120 and 142 chaussée d'Ixelles ☎ 02 511 7504 🕓 Mon–Sat 10–6 🚋 54, 71

FROMAGERIE MAISON BAGUETTE– GASPARD

A master cheese-seller with an amazing array of cheeses, particularly French and Belgian, many made by monks in Belgian abbeys.
🞧 F7 ✉ 28 rue de la Longue Vie, Ixelles ☎ 02 511 7095 🚇 Porte de Namur/Naamsepoort 🚋 34, 80

GALERIE VANDERKINDERE

This expensive auction house specializes in art and objects from the 17th and 18th centuries.
🞧 D9 ✉ 685–687 chaussée d'Alsemberg, St.-Gilles ☎ 02 344 5446 🕓 Mon–Fri 9–12, 2–5. Phone for times of sale 🚋 38; tram 23, 55, 38

GRETA MARTA

Greta Halfin's wonderful, hip store that stocks Von Furstenberg's wrap dresses, as well as young designers she likes such as Stephen Fairchild and Stella Cadente.
🞧 E9 ✉ 58 rue de l'Aqueduc, Ixelles ☎ 02 534 8824 🕓 Mon 12–6.30, Tue–Sat 10–6.30 🚋 Tram 81, 82

MATONGÉ

Matongé takes its name from an area in Kinshasha, in Zaïre, the former Belgian Congo, and it's by far the city's most exotic district. At the heart of it is the Galerie d'Ixelles, between the *chaussées* de Wavre and d'Ixelles. The shops sell African beauty products, foods, fashion and music. The pedestrian rue Longue Vie has several lively African bars and restaurants. At the split of the two *chaussées* is a wonderful giant mosaic by the Zairean artist Chéri Samba, worth the excursion.

SOUTH BRUSSELS

SHOPPING

IDEB LIFESTORE

www.ideb.be

This is a wonderful and luxurious department store in a grand house with sweeping stairways. It is where the *Ixellois* hang out on the weekends to shop for the latest carefully selected fashion for men, women and the house, as well as beauty products and books. When you have finished shopping, take a break in the restaurant, bar or beauty room.

➕ E7 ✉ 49 boulevard de Waterloo ☎ 02 289 1110 🕐 Mon–Fri 10.30–7, Sat 11–7 🚇 Louise

LOOK 50

The oldest vintage store in Brussels has an excellent selection of secondhand clothes and accessories from the 1950s to 1980s. All are at very reasonable prices. In the same street are several other vintage stores, as well as other quaint little boutiques.

➕ F7 ✉ 10 rue de la Paix ☎ 02 512 2418 🕐 Mon–Sat 10–6 🚇 Porte de Namur/ Naamsepoort

MARCHÉ PLACE DU CHÂTELAIN

This delightful square has a good selection of restaurants and bars that are perfect for a lunch stop. On Wednesday afternoons, between 2pm and 7pm, food-lovers flock here for the city's best food market, with fine charcuterie, cheeses, home-made jams, wines and delicious pastries.

➕ E–F9 ✉ Place du Châtelain 🕐 Wed 2–7 🚊 Tram 91, 92 from place Louise

OLIVIER STRELLI

www.strelli.be

Streamlined, modern fashion for men and women in blacks, beiges, greys and browns, with an occasional dash of colour.

➕ E8 ✉ 72 avenue Louise ☎ 02 512 5607 🕐 Mon–Sat 10–6.30 🚇 Louise 🚊 Tram 93, 94

LES PRÉCIEUSES

www.lesprecieuses.com

The Spanish jewellery designer Pili Collado creates striking jewellery with pearls, Bohemian glass and amazing beads

QUARTIER DU CHÂTELAIN

The quiet streets and elegant art nouveau houses in this district attract a young crowd, and the area around the place du Châtelain is fast becoming a trendy shopping hub. There is a picturesque food market on Wednesday afternoons on the square, and some trendy restaurants and interesting fashion boutiques, including Greta Marta (▷ 57), have opened in the streets adjoining the square, such as rue de l'Aqueduc, rue Simonis, rue du Page and rue Faider.

and ribbons. In her shop she also sells handbags and other accessories of talented designers she likes.

➕ E10 ✉ 20 place Georges Brugman ☎ 02 343 9279 🕐 Mon–Sat 10.30–6.30 🚊 Tram 91, 92

SENTEURS D'AILLEURS

www.senteursdailleurs.com

A sumptuous boutique with a selection of the perfumes, home fragrances and skincare items made by perfumers who don't cater to the mass market. Needless to say, the shop smells divine and has a totally relaxing atmosphere. If the choice is too overwhelming, the staff are all experts who trained as 'noses' and can assist in finding something that suits you to perfection.

➕ F8 ✉ 94 avenue Louise ☎ 02 511 6969 🕐 Mon–Fri 10–6.30, sat 10–7 🚇 Louise

SERNEELS

www.serneels.be

A spacious shop with a wonderful, but expensive, range of traditional and contemporary toys, from tiny ducklings to full-size cars and fine rocking horses.

➕ E8 ✉ 69 avenue Louise ☎ 02 538 3066 🕐 Mon–Sat 9.30–6.30 🚇 Louise 🚊 Tram 93, 94

Entertainment and Nightlife

CONWAYS
www.conways.be
All things American are available at this lively bar-grill with superb hamburgers and Tex-Mex cuisine, and giant screens showing football matches. Every night around 11pm the staff start dancing on the bar and the music is turned up by the resident DJ. There are themed parties on special days like Valentine's day, 4th July or Halloween, and every Thursday is Ladies' Night, with half-price cocktails for the girls.
➕ E7 ✉ 10 avenue de la Toison d'Or ☎ 02 511 2668 ◷ Daily from 6pm Ⓜ Porte de Namur/ Naamsepoort

FLAGEY
www.flagey.be
Wonderful arts centre in the old art deco style state TV buildings, shaped like a cruise liner, which often has performances of jazz or world music. Also has Brussels' most comfortable cinema, showing classic films.
➕ G8 ✉ place Flagey, Ixelles ☎ 02 641 1020 🚌 38, 71; tram 81

FOREST NATIONAL
www.forestnational.be
One of Belgium's largest venues draws many major bands and stars, despite the bad acoustics and endless parking problems.
➕ B12 ✉ 36 avenue du Globe, Forest ☎ 0900 00991 🚌 48, 54; tram 18, 52

MILK CLUB
www.milkclub.be
Excellent DJs play at this venue, with its white décor and neon lights.
➕ F8 ✉ 40 rue de Livourne ☎ 02 534 2667 ◷ Fri 11–6 🚋 Tram 93, 94 from place Louise

SOUNDS JAZZ CLUB
Great jazz café that regularly features the best international and local jazz musicians. Near place Ferdinand Lecocq, which is stocked with good bars.
➕ F7 ✉ 28 rue de la Tulipe, Ixelles ☎ 02 512 9250 ◷ Mon–Sat 7pm–1am Ⓜ Porte de Namur/ Naamsepoort

STUDIO 44
www.studio44.be
Belgium's star DJs appear at this funky venue, in the

BELGIUM DANCES

Belgium's reputation for contemporary dance has flourished since Frenchman Maurice Béjart founded his Twentieth Century Dance Company and the Mudra school in 1953—and revolutionized dance in the country. There are now more than 50 companies in residence in Brussels, most of them very contemporary. Anne Theresa de Keersmaeker took over Béjart's company, now called Rosas, and regularly performs around the world.

upper town, with a low key setting and a rather more glamorous crowd. Thursday's 'Stardust Nights' are free, and on Sundays Funk rules on their 'Funky Fever Evenings'.
➕ E7 ✉ avenue de la Toison d'Or 🚋 Thu–Sun from 10.30pm Ⓜ Louise or Porte de Namur/Naamsepoort

STYX
A small repertory cinema with films in the original language, often English.
➕ F7–8 ✉ 72 rue de l'Arbre Bénit, Ixelles ☎ 02 512 2102 Ⓜ Porte de Namur/ Naamsepoort

THÉÂTRE 140
www.theatre140.be
Good venue for international performances of dance, drama, music and regular English-language stand-up comedy.
➕ J4 ✉ 140 avenue Eugène Plasky, EU Quarter ☎ 02 733 9708 🚌 Tram 23, 90

LE TAVERNIER
www.le-tavernier.be
This lively bar has a huge terrace area and indoor space, but it is still hard to find a place to sit. Most regulars tend to hang out at the bar, or dance the early hours away on weekends.
➕ G8–9 ✉ 445 chaussée de Boondael ◷ Daily 10am–early morning 🚌 Tram 81-82

Restaurants

PRICES

Prices are approximate, based on a 3-course meal for one person.
€€€ over €45
€€ €20–€45
€ under €20

L'AMADEUS (€€)

A romantic wine and oyster bar/restaurant in the former studio of the sculptor Auguste Rodin. It's a popular hangout for the sophisticated Ixelles crowd, particularly for Sunday brunch. There's an excellent wine list and an extensive menu including both modern and more traditional Belgian dishes.

➕ E8 ✉ 13 rue Veydt
☎ 02 538 3427 🕐 Tue–Fri, Sun 12–2.30, 7pm–1am, Mon, Sat 7pm–1am 🚇 Louise
🚋 Tram 91, 92

AUX MILLE ET UNE NUITS (€€)

www.aux-mille-et-une-nuits.be
This Tunisian restaurant stands out in an area packed with North-African eateries. Inside, it is an interpretation of a tent in the desert, with fairy lights replacing the stars in the sky. The food, from the salads and little pies to the couscous with caramelized lamb and onions, is delicious.

➕ D8 ✉ 7 rue de Moscou
☎ 02 537 4127
🕐 Mon–Sat 12–3, 6–11.30
🚇 Porte de Hal/Hallepoort

BELGO BELGE (€€)

www.belgobelge.be
In this contemporary Belgian restaurant you can sample the country's traditional fare with an elegant modern twist. The setting is hip and the prices moderate.

➕ F7 ✉ 20 rue de la Paix
☎ 02 511 1121
🕐 Mon–Fri lunch, dinner Sat, Sun 🚇 Porte de Namur/Naamsepoort

BRASSERIE VERSCHUEREN (€)

This archetypal Brussels brown café has art deco touches and a great beer selection. It attracts lots of regulars.

➕ D8 ✉ 11 parvis de St.-Gilles ☎ 02 539 4068
🕐 Daily 8am–2am or later
🚇 Parvis de St.-Gilles

SAINT BONIFACE

The picturesque art nouveau district of St.-Boniface is flourishing again after too many years of neglect. Focused around the church and the well-established l'Ultime Atome (▷ 62) are now several trendy eateries, including the excellent French brasserie Saint-Boniface, the Asian Eat & Love (▷ this page) and Citizen (hot Thai and Vietnamese food). Most places have terraces on the pretty square, so it's a great place to sit on a nice day.

CAFÉ BELGA (€)

Huge bar-restaurant in the old cruise-liner-shaped television building (▷ 59) overlooking the lake in Ixelles. The large terrace is a good place for breakfast, or a drink before a movie.

➕ G8 ✉ 18 place Flagey
☎ 02 640 3508 🕐 Sun–Thu 8am–2am, Fri–Sat 8am–3am
🚌 38, 71; tram 81

CHEZ MARIE (€€–€€€)

This trendy one-Michelin-star restaurant serves delectable French-Belgian food. The wine list is one of the city's finest and the two-course lunch is good value.

➕ G9 ✉ 40 rue Alphonse de Witte ☎ 02 644 3031
🕐 Tue–Fri lunch, dinner; Sat dinner 🚌 71; tram 81

EAT & LOVE (€€)

Trendy Asian eatery in a street that is fast becoming a magnet for good simple restaurants and cute little boutiques. The menu is mixed Thai and Vietnamese, both authentic and equally well prepared.

➕ F7 ✉ 11 rue St.-Boniface
☎ 02 513 6473 🕐 Mon–Fri lunch, dinner, Sat dinner
🚇 Porte de Namur/Naamsepoort

LE FILS DE JULES (€€)

Popular Basque restaurant serving delicious cuisine from southwest France in a very stylish setting. Reservations are essential.

🔲 E9 ✉ 37 rue du Page
☎ 02 534 0057 ⏰ Mon–Thu
lunch, dinner, Fri, Sat dinner
🚊 54, tram 81

LE FRAMBOISIER DORÉ (€)

The most delicious sorbets in town, home-made in the traditional way, and with a wealth of tastes, including *speculoos*, the Belgian version of gingerbread.
🔲 F9 ✉ 35 rue du Bailli
☎ 02 647 5144 ⏰ Tue–Fri
11.30–11, Sat, Sun 12.30–11

GIOCONDA STORE CONVIVIO (€–€€)

A lively restaurant attached to an Italian wine and delicatessen store, serving tasty pasta dishes. The waiters are friendly and entertaining.
🔲 E9 ✉ 76 rue de l'Aqueduc
☎ 02 539 3299 ⏰ Mon–Sat
lunch, dinner 🚊 54; tram 81

LE HASARD DES CHOSES (€€)

Lively and deservedly popular Mediterranean restaurant serving big plates of tasty salads and pastas. The décor is simple but attractive and the terrace at the back is open in summer.
🔲 E9 ✉ 31 rue du Page
☎ 02 538 1863 ⏰ Mon–Fri
lunch, dinner, Sat, Sun dinner
🚊 54; tram 81

L'HORLOGE DU SUD (€–€€)

Lively West African restaurant with Congolese and Senegalese dishes, which include a lot of fish, yams and vegetables. Try the exotic cocktail with baobab juice, which is apparently good for the soul.
🔲 F–G7 ✉ 141 rue du Trône
☎ 02 512 1864 ⏰ Mon–Fri
11am–midnight, Sat 5pm–2am, Sun 5pm–midnight
🚇 Trône

MAISON ANTOINE (€)

Generally regarded as the best *frietkot* in Brussels, a stall with cones of delicious 'Belgian' fries and a wide range of sauces and meaty accompaniments, which are allowed to be consumed in the cafés around the square.
🔲 H7 ✉ place Jourdan
⏰ 11.30am–2am
🚇 Schuman

LA QUINCAILLERIE (€€€)

www.quincaillerie.be
An elegant and delightful restaurant in an old

hardware store, a short walk from the Horta Museum (▷ 52). La Quincaillerie specializes in fish and seafood, serving huge platters of seafood, but you'll also find other delights of the Belgian and French kitchen.
🔲 E9 ✉ 45 rue du Page
☎ 02 533 9833
⏰ Mon–Fri lunch, dinner; weekend dinner only 🚇 Porte de Hal/Hallepoort 🚊 Tram 81, 82, 84, 92

TAGAWA (€€€)

The best Japanese food in Brussels, at a reasonable price. The sushi is divine and other dishes are prepared by the chefs at your table.
🔲 F9 ✉ 279 avenue Louise
☎ 02 640 5095 ⏰ Mon–Fri
lunch, dinner; Sat dinner
🚇 Louise 🚊 Tram 94

L'ULTIME ATOME (€€)

A brasserie that is both trendy and traditional, with a large variety of beers and other drinks, simple but good Belgian dishes and long opening hours. Very popular on weekends, when locals come for breakfast and lunch. Enjoy a coffee on the terrace when the sun shines on this atmospheric little square.
🔲 F7 ✉ Rue St-Boniface
☎ 02 513 4884 ⏰ Mon–Thu
8.30am–12.30am, Fri, Sat 9am–1am, Sun 10am–12.30am
🚇 Porte de Namur/Naamsepoort

Bruges never fails to impress, with its romantic canals, quaint cobbled streets, medieval façades, bridges and towers and amazing collection of Flemish masters.

KOMVEST WALWEINSTR
St-Jozef-kliniek
Sinte-Claradreef
ST-GILLIS
KON ELISABETHLAAN
Dominicanessen
Kon-Atheneum
Elf Julistr
Blokstr
Biezenstr
VLAMINGDAM SINT-JORISSTRAAT
Sinte-Clarastraat
Hoedemakersstr
Ezelpoort
Annuntiantenstr
Klaverstraat
Ezelstraat
Bidderssstr
Couden
Anglikaansekerk
H Losschaertstr
Augustijnenrei
J Bonlistr
Karmelietenkerk
Rozenstr
Zakse
Poitevinstr
GULDEN - VLIESLAAN
Groenstr
Jezuitenkerk
Woensdag markt
Raamstr
VLAMINGSTR
GULDEN VLIESBRUG
Beenhouwersstraat
Crauwerkersstr
Korstr
Jan van Eyckplein
ZaK
Sint-Jakobsstr
HOEFIJZERLAAN
Oude St-Jakobskerk
St-Janstr
Leeuwstr
Stadspark Sebrechts
Chocolate Museum
Stedelijk Conservatorium
Philip-stockstr
Mortierstr
Moostraat
Geld-muntstr
Eiermarkt
Heilig Bloedbasiliek
Muntplein
Proosdij
Brandstr
Lane
Wulfhagestr
Markt
Burg
Guido Gezelle laan
Paalstr
Noord-zandstraat
Zilverstr
Belfort en Hallen
Woelsstr
Huiden-vettersplein
Steenstr
Dijver
Buiten de Smedenpoort
SMEDENSTR
Oude Burg
Arentshuis
Eekhoutstr
KONING
Zuidzandstr
Kathedraal St-Salvator
Gruuthuse Museum
Groeninge Museum
Beursshalle
Maagdestr
Hendrik
Hauwerstr
ALBERT
Bisschoppelijk Paleis
Mariastr
De Vesten en Poorten
Kapucijnen
Arch museum
Onze-Lieve-Vrouwekerk
Conscienceelaan
LAAN
Concert-gebouw
St-Jan Kunstcentrum
St-Janshospitaal en Memling Museum
Zonneke Meers
Boeverielaan
Sint-Gode-lieve-abdij
Westmeers
Oostmeers
Begijnhof
Wijngaardstr
Diamantmuseum
Oude
Boeverlepoort
Brewery Halve Maan
Arsenaalstr
Katelijnestraat
Vlamingstr
Wijngaard-plein
Kliniek Minnewater
Minnewater-park
Minnewater
KATELIJNEBRUG
0   250 m
0   250 yds
BUITEN BEGIJNENVEST
BUITEN KATELIJNEVEST
a   b

Vlotkom

WARANDEBRUG
Handelskom
BRANDWEER

ST-LEONAR-
DUSBRUG
Sasplein

Komvest

I en M Sabbesstr
Kalvariebergstr
S'Gravenstr
Stokersstr

Wulpenstr

**Museum-Onze-Lieve-
Vrouw ter Potterie**

O L Vrouw van de
Potterie Kerk

BUITEN KRUISVEST

Oost Prootse

Peterseliestraat

Langerei

Pottentrei

Bisschoppelijk
Seminarie

Oliebaan

Hotel-en Toerisme-
school Spermalie

Sint-Janshuysmolen

Kazerne

Sint
Gilliskerk

Pottentrei

Gotje
E Zorghstr

Snaggaardstraat

Kazerne

Kadaster
Handstr

Langerei

Rijkepdstr

Ropeerdstr

Carmersstraat

Engels
Klooster

Guido
Gezelle-
museum

Rolweg

Kruisvest

**Museum voor
Volkskunde**

Kant-
centrum

Verrieststr

Centhof

Spinolarei

Sint-Annarei

Verversdijk

Sint-Annakerk

Jeruzalemkerk

Schuttersgilde
Sint-Joris

Peperstraat

Kruispoort

**Sint-
Walburgakerk**

Rodestr

immerr
maalsst

Molen
meers

Verb Nieuwland

LANGESTR

Gerechtshof

HOOGSTR

LANGESTR

KRUISPOORTBRUG

Balsemboomstr

Vismarkt

Rozenhoedkaai

Predikherenstr

Rijkswacht

Predikherenrei

Couture

Vulderstr

Kwekersstr

Billske

BUITEN KAZERNEVEST

Waalsestr

Eerste Leer
touwerstr

Zwarte Leer
touwerstr

Bilske

Moerkerkstr

Kazernevest

**Koningin-
Astridpark**

Vizier
str

Hoogstuk

St-Magda-
lenakerk

Capaardstr

Willemijnendreef

Vollerstr

Garenmarkt

Gentpoortstr

Boninvest

BUITEN BONINVEST

Jakobvnessenstr

GENTPOORTBRUG

Gentweg

BUITEN GENTPOORTVEST

Gentpoortvest

c   d

Bruges

HIGHLIGHTS

● The square
● Statue of Our Lady of Spermalie
● *Béguine's* house

TIPS

● The square is particularly beautiful in early spring, abloom with daffodils.
● Next to the Begijnhof is the equally picturesque Minnewater (▷ 85), the so-called Lovers' Lake, lined with trees.

A haven of tranquillity, the fine enclosed square of the Begijnhof is one of the oldest in Belgium, and one of Bruges' most picturesque corners.

Closed court From the 12th century onward, single or widowed pious women started living together in communities, often after losing their men to the Crusades. They took vows of obedience to God and spent their days praying and making lace for a living. Their cottages were built around a courtyard and surrounded by walls. There were many of these *Begijnhoven* *(Béguinages)*, but the one in Bruges is the best preserved. Since 1927, the Bruges Begijnhof has been occupied by Benedictine nuns, whose severe black-and-white habits are a reminder of those of the *béguines* who once lived there.

The church Several times a day the nuns walk to the church through the green garden at the side of the square. The simple church (1605) is dedicated to St. Elisabeth of Hungary, whose portrait hangs above the entrance. She also appears in a painting by Bruges master Lodewijk de Deyster (1656–1711). The most important work is the statue of Our Lady of Spermalie (c1240), the oldest statue of the Virgin in Bruges. On the left wall as you face the altar is a superb statue of Our Lady of Good Will. The remarkable alabaster sculpture of the Lamentation of Christ at the High Altar dates from the early 17th century.

A béguine's house The tiny museum near the gate, a reconstruction of a 17th-century *béguine's* house, complete with furniture and household goods, gives an idea of how this community lived.

THE BASICS

✚ b4
✉ Wijngaardplein
☎ 050 36 01 40
🕐 Church and Begijnhof daily 9–6.30. Museum Mon–Sat 10–12, 1.45–5, Sun 10.45–12, 1.45–5
🚌 1, 2
♿ Good
💷 Free. Museum inexpensive
➡ Memling Museum (▷ 80)

67

HIGHLIGHTS

● Gothic Room in the
Town Hall
● Town Hall façade
● Mantelpiece of Charles V
in Brugse Vrije museum
● Heilig Bloed Basiliek
(▷ 83)
● Toyo Ito's Architectural
Pavilion

TIP

● Admire the square at
night, when the crowds
have gone.

**This historic enclave evokes medieval
Bruges better than any other part of
the city. Its impressive buildings once
contained the offices of the church, city,
county and judicial authorities.**

A separate entity Until the 18th century, the Burg
was walled in and locked with four gates. The
north side of the square was dominated by the
10th-century St. Donatian's Church, sold by
auction and torn down soon after in 1799. (Under
the trees, there is a scale model of the church,
and some of its foundations can be seen in the
basement of the Holiday Inn hotel.)

The square The whole of the square's west side
was once the Steen, an impressive 11th-century
tower; only the porch beside the stairs to the

Clockwise, from top left: Bruges' Town Hall is the oldest in Belgium; visitors enjoy a horse-and-cart tour of the Burg; ornate carvings decorate the buildings surrounding the historic square

Basilica of the Holy Blood (▷ 83) remains. On the southeast side of the square is the Flemish-Renaissance Civil Recorders' House (1535–37). On the eastern side of the square is the Palace of the Brugse Vrije (1722–27), a rural region along the coast that was subordinate to Bruges. Inside the palace is the *Mantelpiece of Charles V*, a Renaissance work of art by Lancelot Blondeel.

The Town Hall Built between 1376 and 1420, Bruges' Town Hall is the oldest and one of the most beautiful in Belgium. Although its turreted sandstone façade dates from 1376, the statues on its Gothic façade date from the 1970s. The Gothic Room, with its superb ceiling, is where Philip the Good called together the first States General of the Ancient Low Countries in 1464; it is now reserved for private functions.

THE BASICS

➕ c3
✉ Burg
🕐 Town Hall (Gothic Room): Tue–Sun 9.30–5. Museum: Brugse Vrije Tue–Sun 9.30–12.30, 1.30–5
🍴 Restaurants nearby
🚌 All buses to the Markt
♿ Very good
💶 Inexpensive
🔄 Markt (▷ 76), Basilica of the Holy Blood (▷ 83)
❓ Concerts in summer

Canal Cruise

Take a relaxing canal cruise within Bruges (left) or a longer trip to Damme (below)

HIGHLIGHTS

● Groenerei
● Meebrug
● The smallest window in Bruges at Gruuthuuse (▷ 74)
● Views of the Onze-Lieve-Vrouwekerk (▷ 78)

TIPS

● Illuminated evening tours, offered in summer, are particularly pleasant.
● There is a junk market alongside the Dijver on Sunday in summer.
● For a longer canal trip, take the boat to Damme (▷ 96–97).

Bruges is often referred to as 'the Venice of the North' and its *reien* (as the Brugeans call their canals) provide much of the city's romantic charm. Taking a boat on the canals is also one of the best ways to explore the heart of Bruges.

Where to start Several companies offer the same canal cruise that can be picked up from various departure points, including the Vismarkt and Dijver. Commentary along the way is given in several languages and umbrellas are offered when it rains. There are regular departures, as the boats fill up, throughout the day (see the side panel for more information on when the boats run).

Highlights to spot The view of the Groenerei/ Steenhouwersdijk seen from the Vismarkt is one of the most idyllic (and often painted) scenes in Bruges. The Meebrug and the Peerdenbrug are two of the city's oldest stone bridges. At the end of the Groenerei is the Almshouse de Pelikaan. The Rozenhoedkaai is another wonderful corner, with rear views of the buildings of the Burg and Huidevettersplein and of the Duc de Bourgogne hotel. Along the Dijver are some of Bruges' grandest buildings, including the Gruuthuuse Museum (▷ 74) and the Onze-Lieve-Vrouwekerk (▷ 78). The canal becomes much more intimate after that and has several wooden medieval houses, before it ends at the Begijnhof (▷ 66), just before the Minnewater (▷ 85), which was the outer harbour of Bruges before the river silted up, cutting the city off from the sea.

Chocolate Museum

Bruges is famous for its many chocolate shops, but this chocolate museum tells you all you ever needed to know about this delicious product, from the history of cocoa to the production of the famous Belgian pralines.

Chocolate history The museum is housed in the grand 15th-century Maison De Kroon, an old wine tavern and later a pastry bakery. The first part of the museum evokes 2,500 years of chocolate history, through an impressive and well-explained collection of more than 1,000 objects illustrating the origins and evolution of the chocolate. The earliest finds date from 600BC, when traces of cocoa were found in terracotta pots used by the Mayas of Colha (now in Belize, Central America), who were believed to drink their hot chocolates with a lot of foam. In 1519 the conquistadores discovered America and also the cocoa drink, which during the 17th and 18th centuries becomes increasingly popular with the European royals and aristocracy. Only much later was chocolate eaten as a bar.

Pralines and tastings The museum also explains how chocolate is made, with particular attention to the differences in ingredients and production processes over the years. At the end of the visit there is a demonstration of how the pralines are made, and how the fillings are inserted with care. To round off the visit there is a tasting of the freshly made chocolates, and you can ask the expert chocolate-maker about his secrets.

THE BASICS

www.choco-story.be

➕ c2–3

✉ Wijnzakstraat 2 (St.-Jansplein)

☎ 050 61 22 37

🕐 Daily 10–5 (closed some days in Jan)

♿ Moderate

HIGHLIGHTS

● *Chocolateros*, 19th-century ceramic vases with a pouring lip and a tube for blowing air into the chocolate to create foam
● Maison De Kroon
● Chocolate tasting

BRUGES

TOP 25

71

Groeninge Museum **TOP 25**

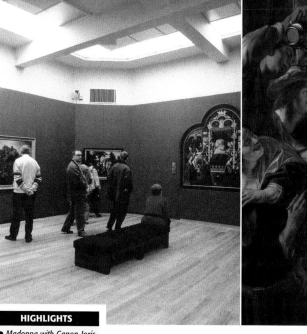

HIGHLIGHTS

- *Madonna with Canon Joris van der Paele*, van Eyck
- *Moreel Triptych* and *Annunciation*, Hans Memling
- *Portrait of a Brugean Family*, Jacob van Oost
- *The Assault*, René Magritte

TIP

- You can buy a combination ticket for €15 that gives entrance to either five museums of your choice (except privately owned museums) or to three museums including bike rental and a drink.

Jan van Eyck's serene *Portrait of Margaretha van Eyck* and Gerard David's gruesome *Judgement of Cambyses*, portraying a magistrate being skinned alive, are so arresting that it is easy to overlook the contemporary art found in this impressive museum.

The Flemish Primitives The 15th-century Flemish Primitives were so named in the 19th century to express a desire to recapture the pre-Renaissance simplicity in art. Room 1 shows works by van Eyck (c1390–1441), including the *Portrait of Margaretha van Eyck*, the painter's wife. There are two works by Hans Memling—the *Moreel Triptych* and two panels of *The Annunciation*—as well as works by Rogier van der Weyden, Hugo van der Goes and the last of the Flemish

Primitives, Gerard David, including his *Judgement of Cambyses*. In Room 7, the 16th-century works of Pieter Pourbus illustrate the Italian influence on Flemish style. In Room 8, look for the lovely baroque *Portrait of a Brugean Family* by Jacob van Oost (1601–71).

Modern Flemish masters Emile Claus (1849–1924) and Rik Wouters (1882–1916) are well represented. Also look for works by James Ensor, Gust de Smet, Gustave van de Woestijne and Rik Slabbinck; works by Constant Permeke represent the best of Flemish Expressionism. There are two paintings by Paul Delvaux and one by René Magritte. The last room shows works by Brugeans Luc Peire and Gilbert Swimberghe, and Roger Raveel and also contains a cabinet by avant-garde artist Marcel Broodthaers (1924–75).

THE BASICS

✚ c3
✉ Dijver 12
☎ 050 44 87 43
🕐 Tue–Sun 9.30–5
🍴 Cafeteria
🚌 1
♿ Good
💰 Moderate
🔗 Markt (▷ 76), canals (▷ 70), Gruuthuse Museum (▷ 74)

Gruuthuse Museum

TOP 25

The museum's eye-catching emblem outside, and porcelain and tapestries inside

THE BASICS

- 🗓 b3
- ✉ Dijver 17
- ☎ 050 44 87 11
- 🕐 Tue–Sun 9.30–5
- 🚌 1
- ♿ None
- 💰 Moderate; Brangwyn Museum inexpensive
- 🔗 Kathedraal St.-Salvator (▷ 75), St.-Janshospitaal en Memling Museum (▷ 80), Onze-Lieve-Vrouwekerk (▷ 78), Groeninge Museum (▷ 72)

HIGHLIGHTS

- Sculpture rooms
- Prayer balcony
- Gombault and Macée Tapestry series
- Illuminated courtyard at night
- Smallest window in Bruges, seen from the Boniface Bridge
- Views from loggia over Reie, Boniface Bridge and Onze-Lieve-Vrouwekerk

The façade and peaceful courtyard of the Gruuthuse Palace take you back to medieval times. It is a delight to stroll around the nearby Arentspark and watch boats glide under the Boniface Bridge, one of Bruges' most romantic corners.

The palace of Gruuthuse Built in the late 15th century by the humanist and arts lover Louis van Gruuthuse, this medieval palace now houses the Gruuthuse Museum, a fascinating collection of antiques and applied arts, well laid out in a series of 22 numbered rooms. There are some fine sculptures, including an early-16th-century Gothic kneeling angel rendered in oak; the impressive *Christ, Man of Sorrows* (c1500), and the 15th-century *Reading Madonna* by Adriaan van Wezel.

Brugean Tapestries Well-preserved 17th-century examples in the Tapestry Room represent the *Seven Liberal Arts*; and some fine baroque wool and silk counterparts in Room 8 have pastoral themes, including the excellent comic-strip-like tapestry the *Country Meal*. Room 16 is the prayer room, in the form of a balcony that looks down into the Onze-Lieve-Vrouwekerk (▷ 78), one of the oldest parts of the building.

Brangwyn Museum (Arents Huis) The Arents House, opposite the coach house, is home to the Brangwyn Museum. Here you'll find the world's largest collection of work by Frank Brangwyn (1867–1956), a British artist born in Bruges.

Kathedraal St.-Salvator

One of the cathedral's Brussels tapestries (below); looking to the high altar (right)

The Kathedraal St.-Salvator, together with the belfry and the Onze-Lieve-Vrouwekerk, towers above Bruges. The splendid sculptures and tapestries inside are a reminder of the cathedral's long and eventful history.

The cathedral A house of prayer existed here as early as the 9th century; it was dedicated to St. Saviour and to St. Eloi, who is believed to have founded an earlier wooden church here in 660. The present cathedral was built near the end of the 13th century. It was damaged by several fires, and in 1798 many of its treasures were stolen by the French, who put the building and its contents up for auction the following year. However, wealthy Brugeans bought a lot back. The neo-Romanesque top was added to the remarkable tower in 1844–46 and the spire in 1871. The oldest sections of the tower date back to 1127.

Sculptures and tapestries The large statue of *God the Father* (1682) by Arthur Quellinus is one of the best baroque sculptures in Bruges. The doors of the Shoemakers' chapel, as well as the sculptures in the Cross chapel and the Peter and Paul chapel, are superb examples of late Gothic oak carving. Six of the eight 18th-century tapestries in the choir and transept, illustrating the life of Christ, were woven in Brussels.

The museum There are wonderful pieces of 15th-century Flemish art among the 120 paintings in the museum, as well as gold and manuscripts.

THE BASICS

⊕ b3
✉ Zuidzandstraat
☎ 050 33 61 88
🕐 Mon 2–5.45, Tue–Fri 9–12, 2–5.45, Sat 9–12, 2–3.30, Sun 9–10, 2–5. Museum Sun–Fri 2–5
🚌 1, 2, 3, 4, 5, 8, 9, 11, 13, 16
♿ Very good
✋ Cathedral free; museum inexpensive
↔ Onze-Lieve-Vrouwekerk (▷ 78), Gruuthuse Museum (▷ 74), Markt (▷ 76)

HIGHLIGHTS

● *Martyr's Death of St. Hippolytus*, Dirk Bouts' triptych (1470–75)
● *Last Supper*, Pieter Pourbus
● 14th-century *Tanner's Panel*
● *The Mother of Sorrows*
● Baroque statue of *God the Father*
● Eekhoute Cross in shoe-makers' chapel
● Eight tapestries by Jaspar van der Borght

Markt

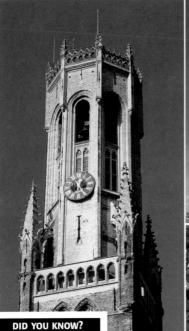

DID YOU KNOW?

- During the Brugse Metten massacre (18 May 1302), Flemish workers and citizens killed hundreds of occupying French soldiers.
- The statue of Jan Breydel and Pieter de Coninck was unveiled three times.
- The Belfry tower is 83m (272ft) high, has 366 steps to the top and leans southeast.
- The tower has a four-octave carillon of 47 bells cast by Joris Dumery in 1748.
- The combined weight of the bells is 27 tons.
- The carillon marks the quarter hour.

The Belfry, emblematic of Bruges' medieval power and freedom, dominates the city's main square, the Markt (Market). The square is ringed with Gothic and neo-Gothic buildings.

The city's core This square, with its attractive historic buildings, has always been at the heart of Bruges. A weekly market was held here from 1200 until it was moved to t'Zand in 1983. The Central Post Office (1887–1921) and the late 19th-century neo-Gothic Provincial Government Palace stand on the site of the former Waterhalles, a huge covered dock where ships moored. Across Sint-Amandstraat is Craenenburgh House, where Maximilian of Austria was locked up in 1488. The square's north side was once lined with tilers' and fishmongers' guildhalls, which are now restaurants.

The Belfry (far left) towers over Bruges' Markt. Climb its 366 steps for wonderful views over the square

Heroes There is a bronze statue (1887) of two medieval Brugean heroes, Jan Breydel and Pieter de Coninck, who in 1302 led the Brugse Metten, the massacre of hundreds of occupying French soldiers by Flemish workers. The same year saw the rebellion of the Flemish against the French king, Philip IV, at the Battle of the Golden Spurs, resulting in Flanders' independence.

The Halles and Belfry The origins of the Halles (town hall and treasury) and the Belfry (called *Halletoren* in Bruges) go back to the 13th century, when the Halles were originally the seat of the municipality and the city's treasury. From the balcony, the bailiff read the 'Halles commands', while the bells warned citizens of approaching danger or enemies. Now you can enjoy Carillon concerts here throughout the year.

THE BASICS

➕ b3
✉ Markt
🕐 Belfry Tue–Sun 9.30–5
🍴 Restaurants and tea rooms nearby
🚌 1, 2, 3, 4, 5, 6, 7, 8, 9, 11, 13, 15, 16, 17, 25
♿ Belfry moderate
🔗 Kathedraal St.-Salvator (▷ 75), Burg (▷ 68), Heilig Bloedbasiliek (▷ 83)
❓ Carillon concerts Oct–14 Jun, Wed, Sat, Sun 2.15–3; 15 Jun–end Sep, Mon, Wed, Sat 9–10pm, Sun 2.15–3

Onze-Lieve-Vrouwekerk

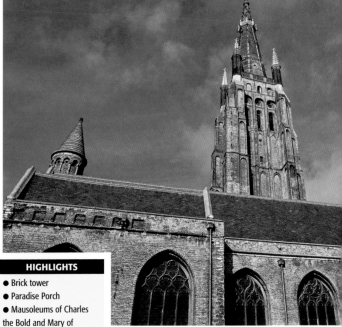

Beneath the monumental brick tower in the Church of our Lady, the religious feeling is palpable, heightened by the aroma of incense, the magnificent sculptures and the stunning paintings all around you.

One of Bruges' seven wonders Although there was a chapel here about 1,000 years ago, the choir and façade on Mariastraat date from the 13th century, and the aisles and superbly restored Paradise Porch from the 14th and 15th centuries. The church's most striking feature is the tower, 122m (400ft) high, begun in the 13th century.

Artworks The star attraction is the *Madonna and Child* by Michelangelo (1475–1564). Other sculptures include a rococo pulpit (1743) by the Bruges painter Jan Garemijn, some fine altars and

The Church of our Lady (left) dates from the 13th century. Inside, see Michelangelo's Madonna and Child (below)

the Lanchals monument in the Lanchals chapel (15th century). The prayer balcony connected to the Gruuthuse mansion (▷ 74) enabled the lords of the Gruuthuse to attend services directly from home. The church contains some important 16th-century Flemish paintings, including works by Gerard David, Pieter Pourbus and Adriaan Isenbrandt. The valuable *Katte of Beversluys*, kept in the sacristy, weighs 3kg (7lb) and is embellished with enamel and precious stones.

Mausoleums Both Charles the Bold, who died in 1477, and Mary of Burgundy, who died in 1482 after a hunting fall, are buried here in superb adjacent mausoleums, moved to the Lanchals chapel in 1806 and returned here in 1979. Excavations revealed beautiful 16th-century frescoes in other tombs.

THE BASICS

➕ b3
✉ Mariastraat
🕐 Church: Mon–Sat 9.30–4.50, Sun 7.30–4.50; no sightseeing during church services. Museum: Tue–Fri 9.30–5, Sat 9.30–4.20, Sun 1.30–5
🚻 1 ♿ Very good
💶 Inexpensive
🔄 St.-Salvator's Kathedraal (▷ 75), Begijnhof (▷ 66), Memling Museum (▷ 80), Gruuthuse Museum (▷ 74), Groeninge Museum (▷ 72)
❓ Weekend services: Sat 5 and 6.30pm, Sun 11am

St.-Janshospitaal en Memling Museum

● On the back of *The Mystical Marriage of St. Catherine*, Memling painted the donors.

● Jan Florein donated *The Adoration of the Magi,* and is shown kneeling on the left of the painting.

● Adriaan Reins, friar of the hospital, is on the side panel of *The Lamentation of Christ.*

The Hans Memling works on show here are 15th-century landmarks in the history of art and are not to be missed. The building that houses them is also a gem.

The hospital St. John's, founded in the 12th century, is one of Europe's oldest hospices (medieval hospitals) and continued until 1976, when medical care was moved to a new building. The Gothic Maria Portal (c1270) on Mariastraat is the original gate. Subsequent buildings include a tower, central ward, brewery, monastery, bathhouse, cemetery (all 14th century), St. Cornelius Chapel (15th century) and a convent for the hospital's sisters (1539). The 17th-century dispensary, with exhibits of remedies, and the church are particularly interesting. The wards were renovated in 2001 and some were converted into cafés and shops.

The Memling Museum was once a medieval hospital

The Memling masterpieces As St. John's reputation as a hospital grew, so did its wealth. Its funds were invested, with inspiration, in the works of Hans Memling, a German painter who had settled in Bruges by 1465 and died one of its richest citizens in 1494. Four of the six works on display here were commissioned by St. John's friars and sisters, the most famous being the *Ursula Shrine* (1489), a relic box in the shape of a church, gilded and painted with scenes from the life of St. Ursula. The triptych *Mystical Marriage of St. Catherine* (1479) was commissioned for the chapel's main altar, as were two smaller triptychs—*The Adoration of the Magi* (1479) and *The Lamentation of Christ* (1480). The diptych *Madonna with Child* (1487) and the portrait of *The Sibylla Sambetha* (1480) were moved here from the former St. Julian's hospice in 1815.

THE BASICS

- ➕ b3
- ✉ Mariastraat 38
- ☎ 050 44 87 43
- 🕐 Tue–Sun 9.30–5
- 🚌 1
- 🍴 Restaurants nearby
- ♿ Very good
- 💷 Moderate
- ↔ Canals (▷ 70), St.-Salvator's Kathedraal (▷ 75), Begijnhof (▷ 66), Onze-Lieve-Vrouwekerk (▷ 78)

De Vesten en Poorten

The round towers of the medieval Gentpoort

THE BASICS

 Gentpoort c–d4;
Kruispoort d3;
Smedenpoort a3;
Ezelpoort b2

TIPS

● The ramparts of Bruges (6.5km/4 miles long) were laid out as parks in the 19th century and are ideal for a good jogging session or pleasant walk.
● Alternatively, rent a bicycle (▷ 118) as there are cycling routes all along.

DID YOU KNOW?

● The statue of St. Adrian (1448, remodelled in 1956) on Gentpoort was carved by Jan van Cutsegem to ward off plague.
● Smedenpoort's bronze skull (hung there in 1911) replaces the real skull of a traitor.
● There were 25 windmills in Bruges in 1562.

To understand Bruges' layout, take a bicycle ride or walk around its walls, especially on the east side, where the gates, ramparts, windmills and canals give the impression of containing the city, as they have done for 600 years.

Fortified Bruges Bruges' original fortifications (de Vesten en Poorten) date back to AD1000, but nothing survives of the six original bastion gates beyond an inscription on Blinde Ezelstraat marking the location of the south gate. Between 1297 and 1300, as the medieval city grew increasingly wealthy, new defenses were built; of the seven new gates, four survive, two in the east—Kruispoort (Cross Gate, 1402), with a drawbridge, and Gentpoort (Ghent Gate, 14th century) with twin towers—and two in the west—Bruges' only two-way gate, Smedenpoort (Blacksmiths' Gate, 14th century) and Ezelpoort (Donkeys' Gate, rebuilt in the 17th and 18th centuries).

Blowing in the wind The eastern ramparts were used as raised platforms for windmills, but only four mills remain between Kruispoort and Dampoort. The first mill when viewed coming from Kruispoort, Bonne Chiere (Good Show), was built in 1888 and reconstructed in 1911, but has never worked. The second, Sint-Janshuysmolen (St. John's House Mill; ▷ 86), near the junction of Kruisvest and Rolweg, was built by bakers in 1770. The third, De Nieuwe Papegaai (New Parrot), a 1790 oil mill, was moved to Bruges from Beveren in 1970. A fourth, built in the 1990s, is near the Dampoort.

BREWERY HALVE MAAN
www.halvemaan.be
The Halve Maan is the only family brewery still working in the heart of Bruges and it's been running since 1856. A brewery tour takes about 45 minutes, after which you can try the delicious local Brugse Zot (Mad Brugean) beer.

🔂 b4 ✉ Walplein 26 ☎ 050 33 26 97 ⏱ Apr–end Sep daily 11–4, Oct–end Mar 11–3 🚌 1, 2 💰 Moderate

CONCERTGEBOUW
www.concertgebouw.be
Finished in 2002 to celebrate Bruges as the European City of Culture, this impressive structure has already become the city's fourth landmark. It has the largest stage in Belgium, and attracts international performances.

🔂 b3 ✉ t'Zand ☎ 050 47 69 99 ⏱ During performances 🚌 2, 3,4, 8, 13, 15, 17, 25

DIAMANTMUSEUM
www.diamondmuseum.be
This private museum tells the history of Bruges as the oldest diamond hub in Europe. The art of diamond polishing was invented in the 15th century by the local goldsmith Lodewijk van Berquem. Diamonds are one of Belgium's main export products and the museum features the imaginary workshop of Lodewijk van Berquem, a replica of the crown of Margaret of York made in Bruges, mining equipment and diamond manufacturing tools used in the diamond industry in Belgium, and thousands of real diamonds. A daily polishing demonstration takes places at 12.15 in the museum's workshop.

🔂 b–c4 ✉ Katelijnestraat 43 ☎ 050 34 20 56 ⏱ Daily 10.30–5.30 🚌 1, 2

HEILIG BLOEDBASILIEK
www.holyblood.org
This is a double chapel, with the 12th-century Romanesque St.-Basilius Chapel downstairs, shrouded in mystery and rich with the atmosphere of the Middle Ages. Even visitors who are casual about religion tend to fall silent in the face of the intense devotion of some of the worshippers. The

Looking down on t'Zand from the Concertgebouw

The annual Procession of the Holy Blood

Reliquary of the Holy Blood is kept in the upstairs 19th-century neo-Gothic chapel. The crystal phial containing two drops of holy blood is contained in a gold and silver reliquary, made by the Renaissance goldsmith Jan Crabbe, richly decorated with pearls and precious stones. One of the holiest relics of medieval Europe, it is believed to have been brought here by Thierry d'Alsace, who was given it by the Patriarch of Jerusalem during the Second Crusade. It is believed that at first the blood in the phial liquefied every Friday, a miracle that stopped in the 15th century, but the chapel is still opened on Friday for the worship of the Holy Blood. The reliquary is carried around the city every year during the Procession of the Holy Blood. The museum contains paintings, tapestries and other silver reliquaries.

✠ c3 ✉ 10 Burg 🕐 Apr–end Sep daily 9.30–12, 2–6; Oct–end Mar daily 10–12, 2–4. Closed Wed afternoon and during services 🚌 All buses to the Markt 🚻 None 👎 Inexpensive ❓ Sun services 8am, 11am. Worship of the Holy Blood Fri 10–11, 3–4

JAN VAN EYCKPLEIN

At the heart of this picturesque square is a statue of the famous Flemish painter Jan van Eyck. At No. 2 is the old Tax House, where the ships coming into Bruges' inner harbour had to pay taxes on the goods they were carrying. It is now an information office. The square overlooks the beautiful Spiegelrei, with some of the city's grandest houses on the canal. In the nearby square of the Woensdagmarkt is a statue of an other Flemish Primitive painter, Hans Memling.

✠ c2 ✉ Jan van Eyckplein 🚌 Bus 6 👎 Free

JERUZALEMKERK

The plan for this 15th-century church was inspired by the Basilica of the Holy Sepulchre in Jerusalem. The remarkable interior includes fine stained-glass windows and the tomb of the Genovese merchant Anselmus Adornes and his wife, who built the almshouses next to the church. Half of the original 12 almshouses have survived, and now form the

Learn how people made a living in days gone by at the Museum voor Volkskunde

Kantcentrum (Lace Centre, ▷ 89) with a good shop and lacemaking workshops.

�–c–d2 ✉ Peperstraat 3a ☎ 050 33 00 72 🕐 Mon–Fri 10–12, 2–6, Sat 10–12, 2–5. Closed holidays 🚌 4, 6 ♿ Good 💰 Inexpensive

KONINGIN ASTRIDPARK

This green zone in the heart of the city is laid out in 18th-century English country style, with a good selection of trees, a pond and a pleasant children's playground.

🔲 c3 ✉ Main entrance Park 🕐 24 hours 🚌 1, 11 ♿ Good 💰 Free

MINNEWATER

South of the Begijnhof (▷ 66) is the Minnewater—the Lovers' Lake. This was the outer harbour before the river silted up and cut Bruges off from the sea. It is named after a woman called Minna who, according to legend, fell in love with a man her father did not like. Minna hid in the woods around the lake, and died there before her lover could rescue her. Her lover parted the waters and buried her under the lake. Next to the lake is a delightful park, with a sculpture garden and free concerts in summer.

🔲 b4 ✉ Arsenaalstraat 🕐 Dawn–dusk 🍴 Café-restaurant 🚌 All buses to the train station ♿ Good 💰 Free

MUSEUM ONZE-LIEVE-VROUW TER POTTERIE

This wonderful little museum is in a former hospital dating from the 13th to 17th centuries. There are sculptures, 15th- and 16th-century paintings, tapestries and furniture. The church has one of Bruges' finest baroque interiors.

🔲 c1 ✉ Potterierei 79 ☎ 050 44 87 77 🕐 Tue–Sun 9.30–12.30, 1.30–5 🚌 4 ♿ Very good 💰 Inexpensive

MUSEUM VOOR VOLKSKUNDE

Bruges' past is recalled in these beautifully restored 17th-century almshouses, originally built for shoe-makers. Period rooms, including an old pharmacy, a shoemaker's work-shop and a small sugar bakery, give an

The beautiful St.-Jakobskerk (▷ 86), founded in the 13th century

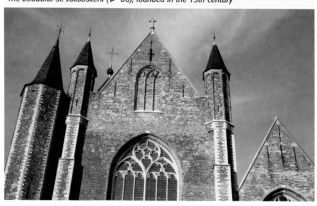

insight into the traditional professions. You can also see the costumes people wore and learn about the popular worship. After the visit, have a rest in the traditional inn ' De Zwarte Kat'.

🔹 c2 ✉ Rolweg 40 ☎ 050 44 87 64 🕐 Tue–Sun 9.30–5 🍴 Medieval inn De Zwarte Kat 🚌 4, 6 ♿ Good 💷 Inexpensive

ST.-JAKOBSKERK

This beautiful church was founded c1240 in a district of rich Brugean families and foreign delegations, who all made generous donations for the decoration of the building. The church has a rich collection of paintings by Pieter Pourbus, Lancelot Blondeel and several anonymous Flemish Primitives.

🔹 b2 ✉ Moerstraat ☎ 050 33 18 34 🕐 Jul–end Aug Mon–Fri 2–5.30, Sat 2–4

ST.-JANSHUYSMOLEN

The only one of Bruges' four windmills that can be visited, St.-Janshuysmolen was built by a group of bakers in 1770 and acquired by the city of Bruges in 1914. It still grinds grain in summer. Inside is a museum.

🔹 d2 ✉ Kruisvest 🕐 May–end Sep Tue–Sun 9.30–12.30, 1.30–5 🚌 4, 6,16 ♿ None 💷 Inexpensive

SINT-WALBURGAKERK

Jesuit Pieter Huyssens built this splendid baroque church between 1619 and 1642, and the 17th-century oak pulpit is astonishing. In summer the church is open to the public at night, with special lighting and music.

🔹 c2 ✉ Sint-Maartensplein ☎ 050 34 32 57 🕐 Easter–end Sep 8pm–10pm and occasionally during the day. Winter: during Sunday services at 10, 7 🚌 6 ♿ None 💷 Free

VISMARKT

The fish market was built in 1821 and fresh North Sea and Atlantic Ocean fish and seafood is still sold here in the morning, from Tuesday to Saturday. The market has a few good fish restaurants, and shops where you can pick up a *stokvis* (dried fish eaten as a snack with a cold beer) or *maatje* (cured herring served with onions).

🔹 c3 🕐 Market Tue–Sat morning 🚌 All buses 💷 Free

A view over the canal from the Vismarkt

Lesser-known Bruges

Discover the canals and quiet medieval streets of this less-touristy corner of Bruges, with its low houses and beautiful churches.

DISTANCE: 2km (1.2 miles) **ALLOW:** 2 hours

START

SINT-WALBURGAKERK
 c2 6

END

BURG
c3 1, 2, 3, 4, 8, 11, 13, 17

1 Start at the Boomgaardstraat, with the baroque church of St. Walburga (▷ 86). Turn right onto the Hoornstraat, then right on Verwersdijk.

8 At the end of the street is Vismarkt (▷ 86), with a fish market. To the right, an alley under the arch leads to the Burg (▷ 68).

2 Cross the bridge and walk along St.-Annakerkstraat to Jerusalemstraat, with the Jeruzalemkerk (▷ 84) to the right. Next door is the Kantcentrum (▷ 89).

7 At No. 47 is the Brewery Museum (☎ 050 33 06 99 ❂ May–end Sep, Wed–Sun 2–6). Before the end of Langestraat turn left onto Predikherenstraat, just past the bridge, and turn right to Groenerei, one of Bruges' loveliest corners.

3 Walk along Balstraat, with the Museum voor Volkskunde (▷ 85). Cross Rolweg to Carmersstraat and turn right.

6 On the corner with Rolweg is a museum dedicated to the Flemish poet Guido Gezelle (1830–99) and farther along, the Bonne Chiere windmill. At the Kruispoort, turn right onto Langestraat.

4 No. 85 is the English convent; No. 174 is the old Schuttersgilde St.-Sebastiaan, the archers' guildhouse; and straight ahead on Kruisvest is the St.-Janshuys windmill (▷ 86).

5 Take a right along Kruisvest.

BRUGES

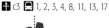 WALK

Shopping

'T APOSTELIENTJE

This small shop offers
professional advice about
lacemaking. You can buy
the tools you need to
make lace, along with
ready-made old and
modern lace.

⊞ c2 ⊠ Balstraat 11 ☎ 050
33 78 60 ⏰ Mon–Sat 9.30–6,
Sun 11–4 🚌 6, 16

BAZAR BIZAR

Plenty of decorative
objects, gifts and
jewellery imported from
all over the world.

⊞ b2 ⊠ St.-Jakobstraat 3/5
☎ 050 33 80 16 ⏰ Mon–Sat
10–12.30, 2–6.30 🚌 All buses

BRUGS DIAMANTHUIS

The technique of
diamond polishing is
attributed to the mid-
15th-century Bruges gold-
smith van Berquem, and
Bruges was Europe's first
diamond city. This shop
keeps alive the tradition
of diamond polishing and
offers a large selection of
quality diamonds and
diamond jewellery.

⊞ c4 ⊠ Katelynestraat 43
☎ 050 33 64 33 ⏰ Mon–Fri
10–12, 1.30–5, Sat 10–3
🚌 6, 16

DELDYCKE

A quality deli with Belgian
specials as well as the
best foods from around
the world, including
cheeses, biscuits, foie
gras and caviar.

⊞ c3 ⊠ Wollestraat 23
☎ 050 33 43 35 ⏰ Wed–
Mon 9–2, 3–6.30 🚌 All buses

DEPLA

www.deplachocolatier.be
This shop, with contem-
porary décor, sells some
of the city's finest handmade chocolates, particu-
larly truffles, florentines,
marzipan and fine choco-
lates decorated with dried
perfumed flowers.

⊞ b3 ⊠ Mariastraat 20
☎ 050 34 74 12 🚌 1

DIKSMUIDS BOTERHUIS

A wonderful shop with
hams and sausages hang-
ing from the ceiling, and
a choice of Belgian and
French cheeses and
breads.

⊞ b3 ⊠ 23 Geldmuntstraat
☎ No phone ⏰ Tue–Sun
10–12, 2–6 🚌 All buses

FABRICS AND LACE

In the 13th century, Belgium
was already famous for
woven fabrics and intricate
tapestries, made from English
wool and exported as far as
Asia. By the 16th century,
Brussels was renowned for
the fine quality of its lace.
Lace remains one of the
most popular traditional sou-
venirs of Brussels and Bruges
but few Belgian women learn
the craft today. As a result,
there is not enough hand-
made lace to meet the
demand, and what there is
has become very expensive.
Many shops now sell lace
made in China, which costs
less but is inferior.

DILLE & KAMILLE

www.dille-kamille.be
A wonderful shop with
simple white household
ware, herbs and spices,
wooden toys and cake
moulds, all at reasonable
prices.

⊞ b3 ⊠ Simon Stevinplein
17–18 ☎ 050 34 11 80
⏰ Mon–Sat 10–6 🚌 All
buses

GRUUTHUSE LACE SHOP

The place to look for fine
lace, especially antique
pieces. All the lace for
sale is made in Belgium.
Handmade porcelain
dolls dressed in antique
lace are another feature.

⊞ c3 ⊠ Dijver 15 ☎ 050 34
30 54 ⏰ Summer: daily 10–7.
Winter: daily 10–6.30 🚌 1, 6,
11, 16

L'HEROÏNE

The best selection of
Belgian fashion is found
at this small but excellent
store, stocking Dries Van
Noten, Kaat Tilley, Chris
Janssens and younger
Belgians such as Frieda
Degeyter.

⊞ b3 ⊠ Noordzandstraat 32
☎ 050 33 56 57 ⏰ Mon–Sat
10–6.30 🚌 All buses

HOET OPTIEK

Funky optician with spec-
tacles 'to be seen in'.

⊞ b2–3 ⊠ Vlamingstraat 19
☎ 050 33 50 02 ⏰ Mon–Fri
9.30–6 🚌 All buses

IKI

Wonderful little boutique
selling good-quality

vintage clothing, jewellery and accessories from the 1920s to 1970s.
🏠 c4 ✉ Katelijnestraat 131 ☎ 0496 938777 🕐 Mon–Fri 12–7 🚌 1, 11

KANTCENTRUM (LACE CENTRE)
See historical and technical exhibits or watch an afternoon lace-making demonstration. Lacemaking materials are on sale.
🏠 d2 ✉ Peperstraat 3a ☎ 050 33 00 72 🕐 Mon–Fri 10–12, 2–6, Sat 10–1, 2–5 🕊 Inexpensive

MALESHERBES
Small shop specializing in good French wines, artisanal foie gras from Périgord in France, home-made terrines and farmhouse cheeses. Next door is a small bistro.
🏠 b4 ✉ 3 Stoofstraat ☎ 0477 74 14 13 🕐 Wed–Sun from 6pm 🚌 1

THE OLD CURIOSITY SHOP
This tiny shop has a very large collection of old postcards, posters, secondhand books and old photographs.
🏠 b4 ✉ Walstraat 8 ☎ 050 34 35 91 🕐 Tue–Sun 2–6.30 🚌 1, 11

OLIVIER STRELLI
A branch of the Brussels' fashion store.
🏠 b3 ✉ Eiermarkt 3 ☎ 050 34 38 37 🕐 Mon–Sat 10–6 🚌 All buses

RAAKLIJN
A good range of foreign-language books, especially paperbacks and art books.
🏠 b3 ✉ St.-Jacobsstraat 7 ☎ 050 33 66 20 🕐 Mon–Sat 9–6.30 🚌 All buses

DE REYGHERE
Books in Flemish, French, English and German, and a selection of international newspapers and magazines.
🏠 b3 ✉ Markt 12 ☎ 050 33 34 03 🕐 Mon–Thu, Sat 8.30–6.15, Fri 8.30–7 🚌 All buses

ROMBAUX
Lovely old-fashioned store with sheet music, CDs and instruments.
🏠 c3 ✉ Mallebergstraat 13 ☎ 050 33 25 75 🕐 Mon–Sat 9–12.30, 2–6.30 🚌 All buses to the Markt

SERVAAS VAN MULLEM
Excellent chocolatier and patisserie, and a great place to sample the best pastries in town or a champagne breakfast.

BELGIAN COOKIES

Pain à la Grècque is a light crispy cookie covered in tiny bits of sugar, while *speculoos* is a finer version of gingerbread. The *coucque de Dinant* is a hard, bread-like cookie that comes in beautiful shapes—windmills, rabbits, peasants, cars and more.

🏠 b2–3 ✉ Vlamingstraat 56 ☎ 050 33 05 15 🕐 Wed–Mon 7.30–6 🚌 All buses

SPEGHELAERE
Bruges' best kept secret, this chocolatier is a far cry from the chocolate shops catering for tourists. All chocolates are made on site; the house special is a bunch of grapes made from marzipan covered in black chocolate.
🏠 b2 ✉ Ezelstraat 92 ☎ 050 33 60 52 🕐 Tue–Sat 8.15–12.15, 1.15–7, Sun 9–1 🚌 3, 13

DE STRIEP
De Striep specializes in comic strips, mainly Belgian and French, but some English. There are also collectors' items.
🏠 c4 ✉ Katelijnestraat 42 ☎ 050 33 71 12 🕐 Tue–Sat 10–12.30, 1.30–7, Sun 2–6, Mon 1.30–7 🚌 1, 11

TINTIN SHOP
www.tintinshopbrugge.be
This shop stocks everything that Tintin fans have ever dreamed of.
🏠 b3 ✉ Steenstraat 3 ☎ 050 33 42 92 🕐 Daily 10–6 🚌 All buses

YANNICK DE HONDT
Stylish antiques shop with a weird but successful mix of 15th- to 18th-century European and Japanese furniture and African art.
🏠 b3 ✉ Mariastraat 12 ☎ 050 34 51 46 🕐 Mon–Sat 2–6 🚌 All buses

Entertainment and Nightlife

CACTUS CLUB
www.cactusmusic.be
The main venue in town for rock, jazz and world music, with the CactusClub@MaZ seating 400 people, and the Cactus@MaZ with standing room for 1,000. The Cactus Club also organizes an open-air festival in Minnewaterpark during the second weekend of July, as well as several other summer festivals in several central locations in Bruges.
➕ a3 ✉ MaZ, Magdalenastraat 27, Sint-Andries ☎ 050 33 20 14
🚌 All buses to train station

CINEMA LUMIÈRE
The Theatre De Korre's two screens feature mainly foreign art-house films and better Belgian productions, without popcorn or advertising. Part of the complex is De Republiek (▷ 92), a café that is hugely popular with locals.
➕ b2–3 ✉ St.-Jacobsstraat 36A ☎ 050 33 48 57 🚌 All buses

CONCERTGEBOUW
www.concertgebouw.be
Opened in 2002, the Concertgebouw aims to attract the best international and national performers in its large and perfectly equipped performance halls (▷ 83).
➕ b3 ✉ 't Zand 34 ☎ 050 47 69 99/070 22 33 02
🚌 1–9, 11, 13, 15–17, 25

CULTUURCENTRUM
www.cultuurcentrumbrugge.be
Seven venues under one name are here, including the recently renovated Stadsschouwburg (▷ this page) and MaZ, a new platform for youth culture. The performances in all these venues include contemporary dance, world music, drama, comedy and classical music concerts, as well as a range of exhibitions.
➕ b3 ✉ St.-Jacobsstraat 20–26 ☎ 050 44 30 40. Box office: 050 44 30 60
🕐 Box office: Mon–Fri 10–1, 2–6; Sat 10–1 🚌 All buses

DOOWOP
The friendly Sadio from Dakar runs his funky Senegalese bar, where the hip hop, funk and soul music, sooner or later gets dropped for African tunes. Often the last bar to close.
➕ c3 ✉ Predikherenstraat 354 ☎ 050 33 54 90
🕐 Daily 7pm–very late
🚌 All buses

KINEPOLIS BRUGGE
Kinepolis is the newest and largest cinema complex in town and has eight cinemas showing mainly original versions of Hollywood blockbusters.
➕ Off map at a4 ✉ Koning Albert 1-laan, Sint Michiels ☎ 050 30 50 00 🚌 27 (weekends only)

LIBERTY
Mainstream films in the subtitled original version are shown here.
➕ b3 ✉ Kuipersstraat 23 ☎ 050 33 20 11
🚌 All buses

STADSSCHOUWBURG
A renovated performance hall staging drama and music.
➕ b2–3 ✉ Vlamingstraat 29 ☎ 050 44 30 60 🚌 3, 4, 8

DE VERSTEENDE NACHT
Intimate, smoky café run by a jazz aficionado. There are free jazz concerts and jam sessions on Wednesday.
➕ c3 ✉ Langestraat 11 ☎ 050 34 32 93 🕐 Tue–Thu 7pm–2am, Fri 7pm–4am

DE WERF
www.dewerf.be
Well-established avant-garde theatre that often stages live concerts of experimental jazz.
➕ b1–2 ✉ Werfstraat 108 ☎ 050 33 05 29

Restaurants

BRUGES

RESTAURANTS

PRICES

Prices are approximate, based on a 3-course meal for one person.

€€€	over €45
€€	€20–€45
€	under €20

DEN BRAAMBERG (€€€)

www.denbraamberg.be
Excellent Belgian cuisine prepared by chef Walter Cosier, who does amazing things with fish. The setting is lavish, and typically Flemish, in a beautiful 18th-century patrician house with a contemporary feel.

➕ c3 ✉ 11 Pandreitje
☎ 050 33 73 70
🕐 Thu–Tue lunch, dinner
🚌 6, 16

BREYDEL-DE-CONINC (€€)

Locals claim this restaurant serves the best moules-frites in town as well as other fish dishes. The decor is nothing special, but the food is really good.

➕ c3 ✉ Breidelstraat 24
☎ 050 33 97 46 🕐 Thu–Tue lunch, dinner 🚌 All buses

'T BRUGS BEERTJE

The place for true beer lovers, with 300 traditionally brewed Belgian beers—many of them rare and for sale only here, and all served in their special glass. The atmosphere is as Belgian as can be. Meals are not served, but you can order snacks and plates of cheese to enhance the beer tasting.

➕ b3 ✉ Kemelstraat 5
☎ 050 33 96 16 🕐 Tue, Thu–Sun 4pm–1am 🚌 All buses

CAFEDRAAL (€€)

www.cafedraal.be
This hidden seafood restaurant to serves waterzooi and an excellent North Sea bouillabaisse, in a splendid setting. There is a torchlit garden terrace.

➕ b3 ✉ Zilverstraat 38
☎ 050 34 08 45 🕐 Tue–Sat lunch, dinner 🚌 All buses

CHEZ OLIVIER (€€)

This homey place is in an old house with fine views over one of Bruges' prettiest canals. The French fare is simple but stylish.

➕ c3 ✉ Meestraat 9 ☎ 050 33 36 59 🕐 Mon–Wed, Fri, Sat lunch, dinner

BEER IN BRUGES

There are two breweries in the heart of town. De Gouden Boom (✉ Verbrand Nieuwland ☎ 050 33 06 99) makes Tarwebier, a wheat beer that's good with a slice of lemon, and a stronger brew called Brugse Tripel with a 9.5 per cent alcohol content. De Straffe Hendrik (✉ Walplein 26 ☎ 050 33 26 97) brews another wheat beer with a sweet aroma.

CHRISTOPHE (€€)

www. cristophe-brugge.be
Belgians eat pretty early, but if you are looking for a place to eat after a film or concert then this is the right address. Cristophe is a great bistro serving Belgian and French dishes with a flair. It's popular so call ahead.

➕ c3 ✉ Garenmarkt 34
☎ 050 344892 🕐 Thu–Mon 7pm–2am 🚌 1

DEN DIJVER (€€)

Dishes here are inventive and lovingly prepared with Belgian beer. The style is old Flemish, and the view from the terrace is tops.

➕ b3 ✉ Dijver 5 ☎ 050 33 60 69 🕐 Thu dinner, Fri–Tue 12–2, 6.30–9.30 🚌 1, 6, 11, 16

L'ESTAMINET (€)

Intimate café with a good snack menu. The spaghetti bolognese is legendary. A busy summer terrace overlooks Astrid Park.

➕ c3 ✉ Park 5 ☎ 050 33 09 16 🕐 Tue, Wed, Fri–Sun 11am until late 🚌 All buses to the Markt

EST WIJNBAR (€)

This rustic wine bar serves snacks to go with the excellent wine, including a cheese platter and a raclette, accompanied by often live jazz or blues music. The garden at the back is open in summer.

➕ b3 ✉ Noordzandstraat 34
☎ 050 33 38 39 🕐 Thu–Mon 5pm–1am 🚌 All buses

DEN GOUDEN HARYNCK (€€–€€€)

The fine chef in this typically Brugean restaurant prepares the freshest ingredients without too many frills. Dishes include pleasant surprises like smoked lobster with fig chutney and scallops with goose liver.

✚ b–c3 ✉ Groeninge 25 ☎ 050 33 76 37 🕐 Tue–Sat lunch, dinner 🚍 1

HEER HALEWIJN (€€)

Old-fashioned and well-known locally, this wine bar with brick walls and lots of candles has an excellent wine list, as well as grills on the open fire and French cheeses.

✚ b4 ✉ Walplein 10 ☎ 050 339261 🕐 Wed–Sun 6.30–10pm 🚍 1

DE KARMELIET (€€€)

www.resto.be/karmeliet
Often regarded as Bruges' best restaurant, De Karmeliet serves the inspired Belgian cuisine of Geert Van Hecke in a stylish mansion with outside terrace.

✚ c3 ✉ Langestraat 19 ☎ 050 33 82 59 🕐 Mon, Tue dinner; Wed–Sat lunch, dinner; Sun lunch; closed 1 Jan–18 Jan

LOTUS (€€)

Originally an organic vegetarian restaurant, now it also serves organic meat at good prices. Open for lunch only.

✚ c3 ✉ Wapenmakersstraat 5 ☎ 050 331078 🕐 Mon–Sat 11.45am–2pm 🚍 All to Markt

OUDE VLISSINGHE (€)

Reputedly the oldest café in Bruges, built around 1515, this is popular with locals as well as visitors. Relaxed and easy-going.

✚ c2 ✉ Blekerstraat 2 ☎ 050 34 37 37 🕐 Wed–Sat 11am–midnight or later; Sun 11am–7pm 🚍 4, 8

DE REPUBLIEK (€–€€)

Large and hugely popular bar with high ceilings, a garden in summer and a good selection of beers and international dishes.

✚ b3 ✉ St-Jacobsstraat 33 ☎ 050 34 02 29 🕐 Daily 11am–1am or later 🚍 All

ROCK FORT (€€)

Trendy new restaurant offering well-prepared Mediterranean dishes with a bit of Belgian and fusion. Attentive service.

✚ c3 ✉ Langestraat 15 ☎ 050 33 41 13 🕐 Tue–Sat 12–2.30, 5–11

BRUGES ANNO 1468

Celebrate the wedding anniversary (3 July 1468) of Charles the Bold and Margaret of York with a gigantic four-course dinner. Beer and wine flow, and minstrels, knights, dancers and fire eaters entertain. Reservations esssential.
✉ Vlamingstraat 86, 8000 Bruges ☎ 050 34 75 72; www.celebrations-entertainment.be 🕐 Apr–end Oct Fri, Sat 7.30pm; Nov–end Mar Sat 7.30pm.

RYAD (€€–€€€)

www.ryad.be
A welcome and exotic addition to Bruges' restaurant scene is this excellent Moroccan restaurant run by the charming Moroccan Mouna and her Flemish husband Philippe. Mouna serves Moroccan food as her mother prepared it for her in Fez, all fresh ingredients and cooked on the spot. The food is really delicious. Upstairs is a tearoom where you can enjoy Moroccan pastries with mint tea.

✚ c3 ✉ Hoogstraat 32 ☎ 050 331355 🕐 Daily 12–3, 6–12 🚍 All buses to Markt

TANUKI (€€)

www.tanuki.be
Classic Japanese dishes in an authentic setting with plenty of wood, a rock-tiled floor and a bamboo garden. Excellent sushi and tempura.

✚ c4 ✉ Oude Gentweg 1 ☎ 050 34 75 12 🕐 Wed–Sun lunch, dinner 🚍 1, 11

T'ZONNEKE (€€)

An excellent rustic yet stylish family-run restaurant serving thoughtful and traditional Flemish dishes. The lunchtime set menu is particularly good value, as is the seasonal gourmet menu at night.

✚ c2 ✉ Genthof 5 ☎ 050 33 07 81 🕐 Tue–Sat lunch, dinner; Sun lunch Sep–end Jun 🚍 All buses

Belgium is not a large country and many of its attractions are just a short train ride from Brussels or Bruges. Marvel at more medieval cities, cycle in the endlessly flat countryside or learn about former battles.

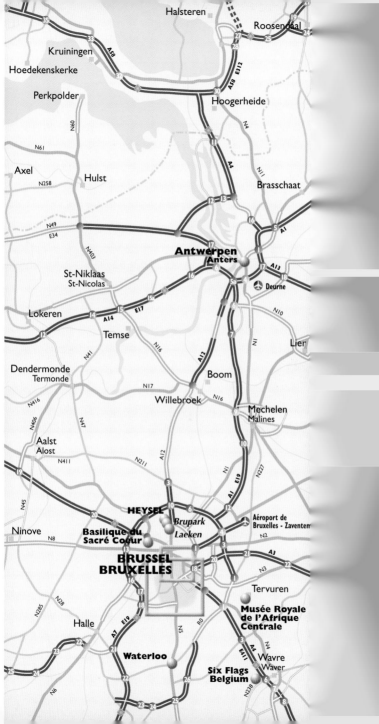

HIGHLIGHTS

● View from the church tower
● Wooden statues of apostles
● A bicycle ride in the surrounding countryside
● A waffle or pancake in a tearoom
● Browsing the bookstores

TIPS

● QuasiMundo (☎ 050 33 07 75; www.quasimundo.com) runs cycle tours from Bruges to Damme.
● Damme has declared itself a book town; you'll find books in French, Flemish and English.

When the port of Bruges dried up in the 12th century, the Bruges-Damme canal was dug and Damme became the city's new port. Sea ships went up to Damme and unloaded the goods on smaller ships to go to Bruges via the canal. The city flourished for the next hundred years.

Missing church Damme's most famous monument, the Onze-Lieve-Vrouwekerk, was built on a grand scale in 1225, but in the 18th century the upkeep costs were considered too enormous, so the part between the church tower and the still-existing part of the church was destroyed, except for the supporting arches—hence the strange shape of the church today. The interior reveals many treasures, including 13th-century wooden sculptures of the apostles and a cross found by

Modern sculpture meets historic architecture (left).
Sunrise over the waters (below)

fishermen from Damme in the sea, outed every year at the Holy Blood procession (▷ 83). The tower gives views over the star-shape ramparts of the city and the surrounding countryside.

Town hall The elegant Gothic Stadhuis of 1464 has two punishment stones on the corner and some fine mouldings inside the Council Hall and the Vierschaere. In front of it, on the main square, is the 19th-century statue of the Flemish poet Jacob van Maerlant.

Food Many Brugeans come to Damme for lunch or dinner, or to have a crêpe after a stroll or a bike ride. The many restaurants offer local fare such as Damme tart with apples, Damme sausages, *anguilles au vert* (river eel in a green sorrel sauce) and a semi-hard Damme cheese.

THE BASICS

Distance 6.5km (4 miles) from Bruges
Journey Time Bus 15 mins

🚌 4 from Bruges' Markt (signposted for Koolkerke)
🚤 The Lamme Goedzak boat runs from Bruges' Noorweegse Kaai 31 to Damme (two-hour excursion) from Apr to mid-Oct, at 10, 12, 2, 4 and 6 (☎ 050 28 86 10)
ℹ️ Huyse de Grote Sterre, Jakob van Maerlanstraat 3 (☎ 050 35 33 19)

Heysel

HIGHLIGHTS

- The Atomium
- Japanese Tower
- Chinese Pavilion

TIP

● Have lunch at the panoramic restaurant in the top sphere, with splendid views over Brussels (☎ 02 475 4775; daily 10–6) or a romantic dinner at Salon '58 (▷ 99). Brunch on a warm Sunday on the terrace is also recommended.

To celebrate Belgium's 100th birthday in 1930, the Centenary Stadium and Palais du Centenaire were built here. But Heysel's most famous landmark is the glitzy Atomium, a pavilion from the World Exhibition of 1958.

The Atomium The Atomium was designed in steel for Expo '58 by André Waterkeyn. Its nine balls represent the atoms of a metal crystal enlarged 165 billion times. The monument (102m/335ft high) remains an extraordinary sight, symbolizing the optimism of its time. It was built to last a year, but it became a Brussels landmark and a symbol for Belgium. At the top is a trendy Belgian restaurant with spectacular views. The ball in the middle has a bar, several other balls are used for temporary exhibitions and one, Kids

World, is dedicated to children. In a nearby pavilion is Salon '58, a trendy restaurant-bar, decorated in 1950s style and offering views of the Atomium.

Exotic landmarks After the Universal Exhibition in Paris in 1900, King Leopold II wanted his own chinoiseries so he commissioned Parisian architect Alexandre Marcel to design the Japanese Pagoda and Chinese Pavilion. The permanent collection in the Japanese Tower reflects the extraordinary interest in all things Japanese at that time in Europe. The Chinese Pavilion houses Chinese porcelain from the 17th to the early 19th centuries.

Trade space The Centenary Stadium hosts sports events and rock concerts, while the Palais de Centenaire forms the core of the Trade Mart, with ten exhibition halls.

THE BASICS

Distance 2.4km (1.5 miles) from the heart of Brussels
Journey Time 25 mins

Atomium
www.atomium.be
✉ Blvd du Centenaire
☎ 02 475 4772
🕐 Daily 10–6
Ⓜ Moderate
🚇 Heysel/Heizel
♿ Few

Japanese Tower and Chinese Pavilion

✉ 44 avenue van Praet
☎ 02 268 1608
🕐 Daily 10–5
🚊 Tram 23, 52
Ⓜ Inexpensive

Musée Royale de l'Afrique Centrale

● Fabulous Central African mask collection

● African jewellery

● Great African food at the restaurant

This fascinating museum, one of the most visited in the country, is trying to shed its colonial image and speed up to a 21st-century view of Africa. It is home to a unique collection of Central African objects, and holds really interesting temporary exhibitions.

TIP

● Read *King Leopold's Ghost* by Adam Hochschild for an insight into the sinister goings-on during King Léopold II's colonization of the Congo.

Léopold's plan The museum had a dubious start. Following the World Fair in 1897, King Léopold II had the idea of founding the Musée du Congo, to illustrate all the 'good' things that Belgium did in Congo Free State. The truth was, however, that Léopold colonized the Congo in 1885 and over the next 20 years plundered the country of everything he could get his hands on, from rubber and ivory to cocoa. He was also involved in slavery, which brought him considerable wealth,

The museum's building (left) was inspired by Paris' Versailles and Petit Palais. Inside, exhibitions include zoology and Central African masks

some of which he used to construct buildings in Brussels, including this museum. The museum was built in 1910, to a design based on Versailles and the Petit Palais in Paris.

Unique The collection of ethnographic objects from Central Africa is the only one of its kind in the world, with a spectacular collection of masks, jewellery, musical instruments and ritual items. There are exhibitions on zoology (including a huge stuffed elephant), mineralogy and agriculture.

Looking to the future The permanent collection has hardly changed since the 1960s, but a large-scale renovation project is due to finish in 2010, making the museum contemporary and dynamic. There will also be a library containing the archives of explorer Henry Morton Stanley.

THE BASICS

Distance 15km (9.5 miles) from the heart of Brussels
Journey Time 1 hour

www.africamuseum.be
✉ 13 chaussée de Louvain, Tervuren
☎ 02 769 5211
🕐 Tue–Fri 10–5, Sat, Sun 10–6
🚇 Montgomery
🚌 107, 110 from Gare du Nord; tram 44
♿ Good
🍴 Cafeteria-restaurant

More to See

BASILIQUE DU SACRÉ COEUR

The basilica's massive green dome is one of Brussels' landmarks, but inside is cold and gloomy. Built between 1905 and 1979 as the world's largest art deco church, it was meant to be a symbol of unification between Belgium's Flemish and French-speaking communities. The views from the dome are superb.

🔆 A1 🖂 1 parvis de la Basilique ☎ 02 425 8822 🕐 Daily 10–6 (until 5 in winter). Dome Mar–end Oct Mon–Fri 9–5; Nov–end Feb 10–4 🚇 Simonis, then tram 19 🎫 Free; entry to the dome inexpensive

BOUDEWIJN SEAPARK

www.boudewijnseapark.be

A great amusement park for both younger kids and teenagers, with Europe's most sophisticated dolphinarium.

🔆 South of Bruges 🖂 12 avenue de Baeckestraat, St.-Michiels ☎ 050 38 38 38 🕐 Apr daily 11–5; May, Jun daily 10.30–5; Jul, Aug daily 10–6. At other times of the year call ahead to check the park is open 🚍 7, 17 from railway station 🛇 Good 🎫 Expensive

LAEKEN

Laeken is home to the royal family, whose palace, the Château Royal, is closed to the public. The exquisite Serres Royales (Royal Greenhouses), with an amazing variety of tropical plants, are open during April and May. Nearby is the pretty Parc de Laeken.

🔆 North Brussels 🖂 Boulevard de Smet de Naeyer 🚇 Stuyvenberg 🚊 Tram 23, 52

BRUPARCK

www.bruparck.com

Bruparck is a mini Europe, with 300 miniature models of monuments in the European Union. There is also a water funpark, Océade, and a huge cinema complex, Kinepolis.

🔆 North Brussels 🖂 20 boulevard du Centenaire, Heysel ☎ 02 474 8377 🕐 Varies 🚇 Heysel/ Heizel 🛇 Good 🎫 Expensive

DE ZEVEN TORENTJES

This former 14th-century farm estate is now a children's farm.

🔆 Southeast of Bruges 🖂 Canadaring 41, Assebroek ☎ 050 35 40 43 🕐 Mon–Fri 8.30–12, 2–4 🚍 2

Vibrant flowerbeds in front of the Basilique du Sacré Coeur

A view of Brussels' spires and sky-scrapers from the Parc de Laeken

Excursions

ANTWERP

Antwerp is a lively Flemish city, famous for Belgian fashion. The ModeMuseum (MoMu) has a historic costume and lace collection, and organizes major fashion exhibitions. Many Belgian designers have a shop in the city.

Not just fashion Antwerp is also the city of Rubens, whose work can be seen at his house, the Rubenshuis, and at the wonderful Koninklijk Museum voor Schone Kunsten (Fine Arts Museum), which has a large collection of Flemish primitives and works from Antwerp's Golden Age (17th century). The Museum for Contemporary Art (MUHKA) features temporary exhibitions. The heart of Antwerp is the Grote Markt square and the Onze Lieve Vrouwe Cathedral, the largest Gothic church in Belgium. The main shopping street is the elegant Meir.

THE BASICS

Distance 45km (27 miles) from Brussels; 105km (65 miles) from Bruges
Journey Time 40 mins (Brussels); 1 hour (Bruges)

www.visitantwerpen.be
🚆 Several trains an hour from Brussels and Bruges
🛈 13 Grote Markt (tel 03 231 0103)

Below from left to right: guildhouses on Antwerp's Grote Markt; reflections of waterside buildings on the Corn Quay, Ghent; mosaics in the Zurenborg district of Antwerp, an architectural conservation area

GHENT

Ghent is pretty much undiscovered compared to Bruges and Brussels, but it's a lively city full of Flemish architecture and art. With a large university, there is a young vibe and vibrant nightlife.

Medieval treasures At the heart of the city is the Gravensteen, the impressive 12th-century medieval castle of the Counts of Flanders. A short walk away is the 14th-century St.-Baafs Cathedral, which hides the city's greatest treasure, Jan van Eyck's *Adoration of the Mystic Lamb*. Across from the cathedral is the Lakenhalle, the 15th-century Cloth Hall, and the majestic Belfry tower, with great views over the city. Along the Graslei are several superb guildhouses.

THE BASICS

Distance 56km (35 miles) from Brussels; 42km (26 miles) from Bruges
Journey Time 40 mins (Brussels); 30 mins (Bruges)

www.visitgent.be
🚆 Several trains each hour from Bruges and Brussels
🛈 Lakenhalle, Botermarkt (tel 09 266 5232)
🍴 Some of the city's best restaurants are in the narrow alleys of Patershol

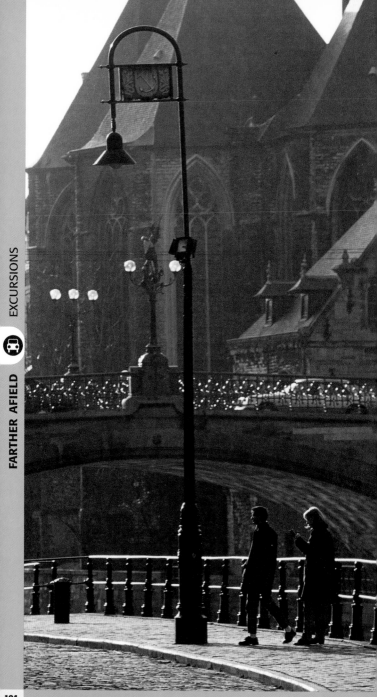

IEPER AND WAR MEMORIALS

During the 12th century Ieper (Ypres) was an important cloth trade hub, together with Ghent and Bruges.

Historic city Many of the Ieper's important monuments date back from that time, including the Cloth Hall, with 48 doors giving access to the spacious halls, the adjacent Belfry (70m/230ft high) and the Gothic St.-Martin's Cathedral. During World War I, the city was bombed for four years and reduced to ruins, while 500,000 soldiers died in the 'Ypres Salient'. The rebuilding of the city took more than 40 years and 170 war cemeteries in the area pay tribute to the fallen soldiers. The Flanders Field Museum tells the story of Ypres during World War I.

THE BASICS

Distance 100km (62 miles) from Brussels; 50km (31 miles) from Bruges

www.ieper.be
www.greatwar.be
🚆 Several direct trains each day from Brussels (1.5 hours) or via Kortrijk (2 hours); from Bruges change trains in Kortrijk (1.5 hours)
🛈 Lakenhallen, Grote Markt (tel 057 23 92 20)

OSTEND

This lively town is popular with Brugeans, who come for a walk along the long beach on weekends, to eat in one of the many fish restaurants around the port or to spend the evening in some of the many bars.

Royal connections The royal family chose Ostend for their summer residence, which earned it the name 'Queen of Belgian Beach Resorts'. Now, the Royal Villa built by Léopold I has long been sold and has become a hotel. Art lovers should pay a visit to the Museum of Fine Arts, which has works by James Ensor and Flemish painters Permeke and Spilliaert. You can wander around Ensor's former house and studio, now called the James Ensor House. The interesting Museum of Modern Art (P.M.M.K.), in an old warehouse, illustrates Belgian modern art.

THE BASICS

Distance 100km (62 miles) from Brussels; 30km (19 miles) from Bruges

www.ostend.be
🚆 Direct train from Brussels (1.5 hours); from Bruges (20 mins)
🛈 Monacoplein 2 (tel 059 70 34 77)

Ghent (left) is a vibrant city, full of Flemish architecture. Ostend (below) is one of Belgium's largest resorts.

THE BASICS

Distance 16km (10 miles) from Brussels
Journey Time 25 mins
✉ E411 Brussels-Namur, exit 6, in Wavres/ Waveren
☎ 010 42 16 00
🕐 Apr–end Oct daily 10–6; Sep Sat, Sun 10–8
🚆 Train from Gare Schuman to Gare de Bierges on Ottignies/ Louvain-la-Neuve line (short walk from station)
♿ Few 💷 Very expensive

SIX FLAGS BELGIUM

Six Flags Belgium, formerly known as Walibi, is a spectacular theme park near Brussels, with a wide range of rides and attractions for all ages.

Feeling brave? Rides include the Werewolf, at 32m (105ft) the highest wooden roller coaster in Belgium, which hurtles you along 1,000m (1,090 yards) of track at an average speed of 80km/h (50mph). Another exhilarating ride is the Cobra, which propels riders at 75 km/h (46mph) into a series of double spirals and through hair-raising loops. Smaller kids have their own area of more gentle rides and can play together with Bugs Bunny and his pals.

THE BASICS

www.waterloo1815.be
Distance 20km (12.5 miles) from Brussels
Journey Time 15 mins
🚆 From Gare du Midi, Central, Nord. Waterloo station is 1km (0.6 miles) from the heart of Waterloo; you can rent bicycles at Braine-l'Alleud station.
🛈 218 chaussée de Bruxelles, Waterloo (tel 02 354 9910)
Wellington Museum
☎ 02 354 7806
Napoleon's Last HQ
☎ 02 384 2424
Visitor Centre
☎ 02 385 1912

WATERLOO

Here is the famous battlefield where the Duke of Wellington defeated Napoleon Bonaparte on 18 June 1815, ending France's military domination of Europe.

Looking back Most people come to see the Butte de Lion (pictured above and below right), a grass-covered pyramid built by local women with soil from the battlefield to mark the spot where William of Orange, one of Wellington's commanders and later King of the Netherlands, was wounded. At the foot of the mound is the Visitor Centre, with the Waterloo Panorama. It is worth climbing the 226 steps for the views. The Wellington Museum, in the inn where the Duke lodged, shows battle memorabilia. So does the museum of Caillou, in a farm where Napoleon spent the night. A motorway now cuts through the battlefield, but for a clearer idea of what happened attend the re-enactment (every five years in June, next due in 2010).

Whatever your tastes and budget, there's plenty of choice for places to stay in Brussels and Bruges. If you haven't already booked your hotel, it's worth checking out the Internet to catch some deals.

Where to Stay

Introduction

Brussels and Bruges have a large choice of accommodation, from the most luxurious to the most simple. Standards are usually fairly high, but quite a few hotels, in Brussels in particular, lack beauty or special character. Most places include breakfast in the overnight rate, but if it is not included, count on paying €10–15 extra.

Brussels As the European capital, Brussels has no shortage of hotels, but most of these are geared towards business people. This means that there are a large number of the smarter chain hotels such as the Hilton, Sheraton, Marriott, Hyatt, Conrad and Novotel. These hotels, and in fact most hotels in town, often offer bargain rates on weekends and during the summer, when the bureaucrats leave town. All year round, but particularly in the spring and autumn, it pays to reserve ahead, as the city fills up quickly. Belgium's central reservation agency, Resotel (tel 02 779 3939; www.belgium-hospitality.com), will reserve rooms for you and check for special offers and discounts. For the impulsive, the Brussels Tourist Office, on the Grand' Place, operates a free same-night booking service.

Bruges There is less need to reserve ahead in Bruges outside the summer months and weekends, but it is safer to do so. Bruges has some very romantic hotels on the canals, which are included in our listings.

BED-AND-BREAKFAST

As an alternative to hotel accommodation, both Brussels and Bruges have an increasing number of charming bed-and-breakfasts. These are usually good quality and less expensive than hotels, and you get the chance to ask the owners for inside information on the best places to visit. Tourist offices can arrange B&B rooms or you can check the list of B&B's on their website. In Brussels, Bed & Brussels (www.bnb-brussels.be) has an online booking service, as has Taxistop (www.taxistop.be).

Budget Hotels

PRICES

Expect to pay under €90 per night for a double room in a budget hotel.

BRUSSELS

LES BLUETS
www.geocities.com/les_bluets
This small and friendly hotel is in a grand 19th-century building. The 10 rooms are decorated with old objets d'art, paintings and mirrors. Smoking is not allowed.
⊞ E8 ✉ 124 rue Berckmans ☎ 02 543 3983; fax 02 543 0970 ⓠ Hôtel des Monnaies

A LA GRANDE CLOCHE
www.hotelgrandecloche.com
There are good-size rooms in this hotel, on a quiet square near the happening St.-Géry area and Grand' Place. The service is relaxed but very friendly.
⊞ D6 ✉ 10 place Rouppe ☎ 02 502 4243 ⓠ Gare du Midi/Anneessens

HÔTEL GALIA
www.hotelgalia.com
A recently renovated hotel, the Galia overlooks the flea market of the Marolles. The rooms, decorated with comic strips, are clean and comfortable.
⊞ D7 ✉ 15–16 place du Jeu de Balle ☎ 02 5024243 ⓠ Porte de Hal/Halleepoort

LA LÉGENDE
www.hotellalegende.com
Attractive and very good-value hotel, with 26 rooms around an internal courtyard. It is ideally located near Manneken Pis and the Grand' Place, as well as the bars and restaurants of St.-Géry.
⊞ D–E5 ✉ 35 rue du Lombard ☎ 02 512 8290; fax 02 512 3493 🚊 Tram 23, 52, 55, 56, 81

PHILEAS FOGG
www.phileasfogg.be
Beautiful, welcoming bed-and-breakfast with five rooms, furnished with antiques, Belgian art and objects picked up by the owner on her travels. Also four studio flats.
⊞ G4 ✉ 65 rue van Bemmel ☎ 02 217 8338 ⓠ Madou/Botanique 🚊 Tram 92, 93, 94

INEXPENSIVE HOTELS

Many hotels in Brussels are business-oriented, so in summer and on weekends prices can drop by up to 50 per cent. The Belgian Tourist Reservations office on Grand' Place (☎ 02 513 7484; fax 02 513 9277) has a free list of more than 800 hotels offering off-peak reductions. Although this makes it difficult to reserve far in advance, hotels are less full in these periods. Alternatively, you could try bed-and-breakfast accommodation (▷ 108).

SLEEP WELL
www.sleepwell.be
Former YMCA with good rooms and dormitory beds at hostel rates. There is no longer a lock-out, and the central location is excellent.
⊞ E4 ✉ 23 rue du Damier ☎ 02 218 5050; fax 02 218 1313 ⓠ Rogier/De Brouckére 🚊 Tram 91, 92, 93, 94

BRUGES

BAUHAUS
www.bauhaus.be
Popular central hostel with free sheets and showers. Part of it is now a one-star hotel, with rooms that have a private shower. There is a very popular bar downstairs.
⊞ d3 ✉ 135 Langestraat ☎ 050 34 10 93; fax 050 33 41 80 🚌 6, 16

B&B MARIE-PAULE GESQUIÈRE
Three comfortable rooms in an ivy-clad house over-looking a park by the city walls and windmills. Very good breakfast with eggs and Belgian chocolate.
⊞ d2 ✉ 14 Oostproosse ☎ 050 33 92 46 🚌 7, 14

IMPERIAL
Seven pleasant rooms on a quiet street in the heart of Bruges. The lobby has antiques and bird cages.
⊞ b3 ✉ 24–28 Dweersstraat ☎ 050 33 90 14; fax 050 34 43 06 🚌 All buses

Mid-Range Hotels

BRUSSELS

AGENDA LOUISE
www.hotel-agenda.com
Friendly service and 38 comfortable rooms, close to avenue Louise.
➕ E8 ✉ 6 rue de Florence ☎ 02 539 0031; fax 02 539 0063 🔟 Louise/Louiza
🚋 Tram 91

ARLEQUIN
www.arlequin.be
A three-star hotel close to the Grand' Place, with 92 comfortable rooms. A buffet breakfast is served in the 7th Heaven dining room, which has views of the Grand' Place.
➕ E5 ✉ 17–19 rue de la Fourche ☎ 02 514 1615
🔟 Bourse/Gare Centrale

COMFORT ART HOTEL SIRU
www.comforthotelsiru.com
The neon-lit exterior brightens up the drab square, but the interior is even more vibrant. The rooms and corridors are mostly modernist, with walls full of bright murals, poems and comic strips.
➕ E3–4 ✉ 1 place Rogier ☎ 02 203 3580
🔟 Rogier

HESPERIA SABLON
www.hoteles-hesperia.es
A modern, efficient

hotel, with 32 rooms.
➕ E6 ✉ 2–8 rue de la Paille, Sablon ☎ 02 513 6040; fax 02 511 8141 🚋 Tram 91, 92, 93, 94

MARRIOTT BRUSSELS
www.marriott.com
Good value five-star hotel with spacious rooms and excellent service, right in the heart of the city, near the shopping and nightlife areas of St.-Géry and Ste.-Catherine and a five-minute walk from the Grand' Place.
➕ D5 ✉ 3–7 rue A. Orts ☎ 02 516 9090 🔟 Bourse

METROPOLE
www.metropolehotel.com
This grand hotel, opened in 1895, has wonderful architecture in the public spaces. The bedrooms

are more simple but comfortable, and week-end rates are good value.
➕ E4 ✉ 31 place de Brouckère ☎ 02 217 2300; fax 02 218 0220
🔟 De Brouckère 🚋 Tram 23, 52, 55, 56, 81

MOZART
www.hotel-mozart.be
In a lovely 17th-century building right in the heart of Brussels, the hotel has 50 rooms in an opulent Louis XV style.
➕ E5 ✉ 23 rue Marché aux Fromages ☎ 02 502 6661
🔟 Bourse/Gare Centrale

MONTY
www.monty-hotel.be
Far from the heart of town but convenient for the EU Quarter and Le Cinquantenaire, this small boutique hotel has 18 spacious rooms, meticulously designed in a modernist warm style. The rooms are furnished with designs by Philippe Starck, Charles Eames, A. Castiglioni and Ingo Mauer, among others, and the colour scheme is elegant. Friendly service.
➕ Off map J6 ✉ 101 boulevard Brand Whitlock ☎ 02 734 5636 🔟 Georges-Henri

NOGA
www.nogahotel.com
Tranquil, charming hotel in the Ste.-Catherine district, near the hip hangouts on the rue Dansaert and rue des Flandres.
➕ D4 ✉ 38 rue du Béguinage ☎ 02 218 6763
🔟 Ste.-Catherine/St.-Katelijne

ST.-MICHEL
www.hotelsaintmichel.be
Family-run, 15-room hotel behind the gilded façade of the House of the Duke of Brabant. Grand' Place can be noisy at night.
🔼 E5 ✉ 15 Grand' Place
☎ 02 511 0956
🚇 Gare Centrale/Bourse
🚋 Tram 23, 52, 55, 56, 81

WELCOME
www.hotelwelcome.com
Family-run hotel in a quiet street near the fashionable area around rue Dansaert. The 15 rooms are decorated in the style of another country.
🔼 D4 ✉ 5 rue du Peuplier
☎ 02 219 9546; fax 02 217 1887 🚇 Ste.-Catherine/St.-Katelijne

BRUGES

ADORNES
www.adornes.be
Quiet three-star hotel in a beautiful old Flemish house overlooking a canal. The rooms are comfortable, and breakfast is served in a lovely room with a fire place. Friendly service.
🔼 c2 ✉ St.-Annarei 26
☎ 050 34 13 36 🚌 7

ANSELMUS
www.anselmus.be
Pleasant hotel in a 17th-century mansion in a quiet street. The spacious rooms are stylishly decorated, and breakfast is good, too.
🔼 c2–3 ✉ Ridderstraat 15
☎ 050 34 13 74 🚌 All to Markt

DE GOEZEPUT
www.hotelgoezeput.be
Delightful small hotel in a quiet street, in an 18th-century monastery. The rooms ooze charm and the cellar-bar is popular with locals.
🔼 b3 ✉ 29 Goezeputstraat
☎ 050 342013 🚌 All to t'Zand

GRAND HOTEL DU SABLON
www.sablon.be
Traditional hotel with stained-glass art nouveau dome and 36 rooms, offering modern facilities. The rear of the hotel was an inn 400 years ago.
🔼 b3 ✉ 21 Noordzandstraat
☎ 050 33 39 02; fax 050 33 39 08 🚌 All

PARKING IN BRUGES
The use of a parking disc is compulsory to park in the heart of Bruges from Monday to Saturday (except public holidays) 9am–7pm, and parking is allowed for up to four hours. Several streets have been reserved for residents' parking. Visitors are encouraged to drop off their luggage at their hotel and then park the car in one of the large car parks in the city (€8.70/24hrs) or the P Centrum car park near the train station (€2.50/24hrs), with a free bus service to the heart of the city. Central Bruges is quite small and most of the sights are easily reached on foot.

HUYZE DIE MAENE
www.huyzediemaene.be
This bed-and-breakfast has just two luxurious rooms and a sumptuous suite but the location is as central as it gets. Reserve in advance as this is a popular spot.
🔼 b3 ✉ 17 Markt
☎ 050 33 39 59 🚌 All buses to Markt

HOTEL MONTANUS
www.montanus.be
Romantic family-run boutique hotel in a 17th-century mansion with an interior garden. There are 20 chic rooms with a luxury feel.
🔼 c3 ✉ 78 Nieuwe Gentweg ☎ 050 33 11 76; fax 050 34 09 38 🚌 1, 11

PRINSENHOF
www.prinsenhof.be
Quiet and sumptuous 16-room hotel decorated in an elegant Burgundian style with chandeliers, antiques, four-poster beds and moulded ceilings.
🔼 b3 ✉ Ontvangersstraat 9
☎ 050 34 26 90; fax 050 34 23 21

RELAIS OUD HUIS AMSTERDAM
www.oha.be
Attractive renovation of two 17th-century houses, furnished with antiques and overlooking a canal. The 34 rooms are individually decorated.
🔼 c2 ✉ 3 Spiegelrei ☎ 050 34 18 10; fax 050 33 88 91
🚌 4, 8

Luxury Hotels

PRICES

Expect to pay more than €150 per night for a double room in a luxury hotel.

BRUSSELS

AMIGO

www.hotelamigo.com
One of Brussels' finest hotels (▷ panel), the Amigo is in the style of an 18th-century mansion. The staff are friendly and the 176 rooms are elegantly furnished. It is popular with ministers and French media stars.
✚ E5 ✉ 1–3 rue de l'Amigo ☎ 02 547 4747; fax 02 513 5277 🚇 Bourse/Beurs, Gare Centrale 🚌 34, 48, 94

CONRAD BRUSSELS

www.conradhotels.com
One of the city's grandest hotels, with 250 stylish and sumptuous rooms, all five-star amenities, some great restaurants and perfect service. It is located at the heart of Brussels' upmarket shopping district.
✚ E7–8 ✉ 71 avenue Louise ☎ 02 542 4242 🚇 Louise

LE DIXSEPTIÈME

www.ledixseptieme.be
Stylish hotel in the 17th-century former residence of the Spanish ambassador. The 24 elegant rooms are arranged around a tranquil courtyard.
✚ E5 ✉ 25 rue de la Madeleine ☎ 02 517 1717; fax 02 502 6424 🚇 Gare Centrale/Centraal Station

HYATT REGENCY BRUSSELS-BARCEY

www.brussels.hyatt.com
This ultra-chic hotel has 99 rooms and suites decorated in rich colours, with textiles and objets d'art that give a homey feeling. The restaurant, Le Barsey, attracts celebrities and artists.
✚ G10 ✉ 381–383 avenue Louise ☎ 02 649 9800; fax 02 640 1764 🚇 Louise, then tram 93, 94

BRUGES

DE ORANGERIE

www.hotelorangerie.com
Nineteen tasteful rooms in a renovated 15th-century convent covered in ivy and

AMIGO

The Amigo stands on the site of Brussels' former city prison, which, like the hotel now, had its fair share of celebrity occupants. The 19th-century French poet Paul Verlaine shot his lover Arthur Rimbaud in the wrist in the street and ended up here, and so did Karl Marx after the police found communist publications in his rooms at the Hôtel Le Bois Sauvage, on the place St.-Gudule.

filled with antiques and objets d'art. The hotel overlooks one of Bruges' prettiest corners and in summer breakfast is served by the canal.
✚ c3 ✉ Kartuizerinnenstraat 10 ☎ 050 34 16 49; fax 050 33 30 16 🚌 1, 6, 11, 16

RELAIS RAVENSTEIN

www.relaisravenstein.be
A unique boutique hotel where the classic architecture of the buildings blends with a contemporary style. Some of the 15 rooms overlook the canal, as does the restaurant's terrace.
✚ c2–3 ✉ Molenmeers 11 ☎ 050 47 69 47; fax 050 47 69 48 🚌 6, 16

ROMANTIK PANDHOTEL

www.pandhotel.com
An 18th-century carriage house hidden in a leafy square, converted into a small and stylish hotel decorated with antiques and objets d'art. The 23 rooms are sumptuous but not overstated.
✚ c3 ✉ Pandreitje 16 ☎ 050 34 06 66; fax 050 34 05 06 🚌 All buses

DE TUILERIEEN

www.hoteltuilerieen.com
A 16th-century mansion with views of the Dijver canal and 45 rooms.
✚ c3 ✉ Dijver 7 ☎ 050 34 36 91; fax 050 34 04 00 🚌 1, 6, 11, 16

Use this section to familiarize yourself with travel to and within Brussels and Bruges. The Essential Facts will give you some insider knowledge of the cities and you'll also find some language tips.

Planning Ahead

When to Go

Belgium has warm summers and mild winters. The country's northern location gives it gloriously long summer nights, perfect for enjoying outdoor cafés. The peak tourist season is July and August, when the crowds add to the buzz in Brussels but can overwhelm Bruges.

TIME
Belgium is one hour ahead of GMT, 6 hours ahead of New York and 9 hours ahead of Los Angeles.

AVERAGE DAILY MAXIMUM TEMPERATURES

JAN	FEB	MAR	APR	MAY	JUN	JUL	AUG	SEP	OCT	NOV	DEC
5°C	6°C	9°C	11°C	15°C	18°C	20°C	20°C	19°C	15°C	10°C	6°C
41°F	43°F	48°F	52°F	59°F	64°F	68°F	68°F	66°F	59°F	50°F	43°F

Spring (April to May) may take a while to arrive, but by May the weather is warmer and sunnier.

Summer (June to August) can be glorious—or cloudy and rainy.

Autumn (September to November) sees mild temperatures, and there can be good, clear days, especially in September and October.

Winter (December to March) has little snow and the temperatures rarely get below freezing, but it rains frequently, sometimes accompanied by strong winds and hail.

WHAT'S ON

January *Brussels International Festival of Fantastic Film* (www.bifff.org).

April *Brussels Film Festival* (www.fffb.be).

April–May Brussels' Royal Greenhouses (Serres Royales) open to the public (▷ 102).

May *Procession of the Holy Blood* in Bruges (▷ 83).
Brussels Jazz Marathon (www.brussels jazzmarathon.be).
Brussels Half Marathon: A run of 20km (12.5 miles) (☎ 02 511 9000; www. 20kmdebruxelles.be/20km).

Summer Festival (May/Jun–Sep): Classical concerts in Brussels.

June Re-enactment of the Battle of Waterloo at Waterloo (mid-Jun, every five years; next event in 2010).

July *Brussels Ommegang* (first Thu).
Cactus Festival in Bruges (second weekend): open-air concerts (www.cactusfestival.be).
Foire du Midi (mid-Jul to mid-Aug): largest fair in Europe, in Brussels.
National Day (21 Jul): Festivities in Brussels.

August Raising of the

Meiboom, or maypole, in Brussels (9 Aug).
Floral carpet (mid-Aug, even-numbered years): on Brussels' Grand' Place.
Reiefeesten or Festival of the Canals (every three years; next in 2008) in Bruges.

August–September *Gouden Boomstoet* or Pageant of the Golden Tree (every five years) in Bruges; next in 2007.

Heritage Days: Hundreds of houses and monuments open to the public in Belgium.

October–December *Europalia*: Arts and cultural events in Brussels.

Brussels and Bruges Online

www.belgianstyle.com
This site includes a guide to Belgian beers, with a description of the different varieties, where they are brewed and sold, the special glasses that go with them, and, of course, a list of the best bars.

www.brugge.be
A site run by the tourist office in Bruges that has practical information, virtual walks through the city, history and recommendations for hotels, restaurants and excursions.

www.brusselsdiscovery.com
The website of the Brussels Tourist Office has plenty of suggestions on how to discover the city over a weekend. Lots of practical information, a few quirky ideas, inexpensive hotel deals and a virtual comic-strip walk—it's all easy to find.

www.frites.be
Flippant webzine in French covering everything Belgian, including the best places to eat *frites*.

www.modobruxellae.be
Modo Bruxellae has details of various Belgian designers and designer sales, as well as a list of the best shops.

www.noctis.com
Listings of bars, clubs, parties, music events and festivals, as well as information for gay visitors.

www.tintin.be
Everything you ever wanted to know about Tintin, Belgium's comic strip hero.

www.toerismevlaanderen.be
This excellent website, run by the Tourism Flanders office in Brussels, offers information on Bruges, Brussels and the rest of Flanders and also gives a bird's-eye view of the region.

GOOD TRAVEL SITES

www.fodors.com
A complete travel-planning site. You can research prices and weather; book air tickets, cars and rooms; ask questions (and get answers) from fellow travellers; and find links to other sites.

www.trabel.com
The award-winning site of Belgium Travel Network has general information about Belgium, but specializes in practical information on car rental, travel, airlines, hotels and nightlife.

CYBERCAFÉS

BXL
➕ E5–6 ✉ 46 place de la Vieille Halle aux Blés, Brussels ☎ 02 5029980; www.bxlcafe.be 🕐 12–12 (until 1am Fri, Sat) 💶 €2 per hour

Easyeverything
➕ E4 ✉ 9 place de Brouckère, Brussels ☎ 02 211 0820; www.easyeverything.com 🕐 24 hours 💶 €1.50–€2.50 per hour.

The Coffee Link
➕ b3 ✉ Congress Centre Oud Sint-Jan, 38 Mariastraat, Bruges ☎ 050 34 99 73 🕐 10–9 💶 7 cents per minute

Getting There

INSURANCE

EU nationals receive emergency medical treatment with the European Health Insurance Card. Obtain one before travelling. Full health and travel insurance is still advised. US travellers should check their health coverage before departure. Full insurance is advised for all other travellers.

MAPS

In Brussels, street names and metro stations are marked in French and Flemish. In Bruges, street names are in Flemish only. Pick up free bus maps (and metro maps in Brussels) and timetables from tourist offices, the metro, the STIB/MIVB office in Brussels' Gare du Midi station and the bus office at Bruges rail station.

AIRPORTS AND PORTS

The international airport is Zaventem, 14km (9 miles) northeast of Brussels. Eurostar trains from London arrive at Brussels' Gare du Midi station. Car ferries and jetfoils arrive at the ports of Zeebrugge and Oostende.

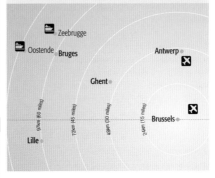

Zeebrugge

Oostende   Bruges

Antwerp

Ghent

97km (60 miles)
72km (45 miles)
48km (30 miles)
24km (15 miles)

Brussels

Lille

ARRIVING BY AIR

Zaventem airport is also known as Brussels International Airport (☎ 0900 70000, available 7am–10pm; www.brusselsairport.be).
The Airport City Express shuttle train (☎ 02 528 2828; www.b-rail.be) takes passengers from the airport to Brussels' main railway stations every 15–20 minutes (🕒 5.12am–midnight; journey time 30 minutes; cost 82.60). The Airport Line (☎ 02 515 2000; www.stib.irisnet.be) has several buses to the heart of Brussels—bus No.12 runs 7am–8pm; journey time 35 minutes; cost €3. De Lijn (☎ 02 526 2820; www.delijn.be) also runs

buses from the airport to the Gare du Nord (🕒 6am–midnight; 45 minutes; cost €2.50). Regular trains leave from Brussels' South, North and Central stations to Bruges (☎ 02 528 28 28; www.b-rail.be) 4.30am–11pm (journey time one hour;

cost €10.90). Taxis outside the airport's arrivals hall display a blue-and-yellow emblem, but they are expensive (around €25 to Brussels). Many accept credit cards; confirm with the driver before you travel.

ARRIVING BY TRAIN
Eurostar trains from London arrive at Brussels' Gare du Midi (journey time 2 hours 40 minutes; www.eurostar.com). Trains to Bruges leave from the same station. The TGV from Paris also arrives at Gare du Midi. Trains connect many major European cities to Brussels, and there are trains from Germany and Holland to Bruges.

ARRIVING BY SEA
P&O Ferries is the only company to run ferries to Belgium—from Hull in the UK to Zeebrugge (www.poferries.com; journey time 14 hours). To drive from there to Bruges take the N31 and N371 (15 minutes), and to Brussels the N31 and E40 (1 hours and 15 minutes).

Eurotunnel takes cars and their passengers from Folkestone to Coquelles, near Calais, in France in 35 minutes (UK ☎ 08705 353535; www.eurotunnel.com; 24 hours with several services an hour between 7am to midnight).

Hoverspeed's Seacat Catamaran (☎ 0870 240 8070; www.hoverspeed.com) no longer sails from Dover (UK) to Oostende, only to Calais (50 minutes). Other companies, like Seafrance and P&O ferries, also make the crossing from Dover to Calais in about 75 minutes. To drive from Calais to Bruges take the E40 (1 hour and 20 minutes); to Brussels take the E15 (2 hours).

ARRIVING BY BUS
Eurolines buses connect major European cities with Brussels (www.eurolines.com). The international bus station is CCN Gare du Nord/Noordstation (✉ 80 rue du Progrès ☎ 02 274 1350). There are direct buses from London to Bruges, as well as frequent trains from Gare du Nord to Bruges.

PASSPORTS/VISAS

Always check the latest entry requirements before you travel, as regulations can change at short notice.

VISITORS WITH DISABILITIES

There are few facilities on buses, trams and the metro for people with disabilities, but a minibus service equipped for wheelchairs is available at low cost from the public transport network STIB/MIVB (☎ 02 515 2365; www.stib.be). On trains outside Brussels, a passenger accompanying a passenger with disabilities travels free.

Few buildings in Brussels and Bruges have facilities for people with disabilities, and the streets have uneven cobblestones, which are tough on wheelchairs. For more information, contact Mobility International (✉ Boulevard Baudouin 18 ☎ 02 201 5608; email: mobint@dproducts.be).

Getting Around

BICYCLING TOURS

● In Bruges several companies offer bicycle tours with a guide, around the city or to the surrounding countryside, including Damme and Oostburg. One of the best is QuasiMundo Biketours (☎ 050 33 07 75; www.quasimundo.com). Others include the Pink Bear Bike Tours (☎ 050 61 66 86; www.pinkbear.freeservers. com) and the Green Bike Tour (☎ 050 61 26 67).
● In Brussels, Pro Vélo organizes interesting bicycling tours with different themes (☎ 02 502 7255; www.provelo.org).

HORSE AND CARTS

Horse and carts, or *calèches,* are a popular way to see the historical heart of Bruges. You can pick one up on the Markt, and the ride usually takes about a half hour, with a little stop at the Begijnhof. The price per cart is fixed at €30. In winter blankets are provided as it can be bitterly cold.

TAXIS

● In Brussels, use only official taxis, with a taxi light on the roof. Taxis are metered and can be called or flagged down. Drivers are not allowed to stop if you are less than 100m (110 yards) from a taxi stand. The meter price is per kilometre and is doubled if you travel outside the city (☎ 02 268 0000 or 02 349 4343).
● In Bruges, taxi stands are on Markt (☎ 050 33 44 44) and at the rail station (☎ 050 38 46 60).

BICYCLES

● The best way to get around Brussels is by bicycle, but watch out for traffic. Bicycles are now available to rent from the tourist office in Grand' Place and can be dropped off at several points in the city. You could also try Pro Vélo (✉ 15 rue de Londres, Ixelles ☎ 02 502 7255; www.provelo.org).
● Getting around Bruges by bicycle is great. Outside the city, Damme is only 6.5km (4 miles) away, and Knokke or Zeebrugge less than 21km (13 miles). You can rent bicycles from:
   ● Station Brugge/Bagage (☎ 050 30 23 29).
   ● 't Koffieboontje (✉ Hallestraat 4 ☎ 050 33 80 27; www.adventure-bike-renting.be).
   ● Eric Popelier (✉ 26 Mariastraat ☎ 050 34 32 62; also has tandems and scooters).
   ● Bauhaus Bike Rental (✉ 145 Langestraat ☎ 050 34 10 93; www.bauhaus.be).
● Major rail stations in Belgium sell tickets for train journey and bicycle rental (✉ 02 555 2525).

BUSES, TRAMS AND METRO IN BRUSSELS

● Brussels' metro stations are indicated by a white letter 'M'.
   Line 1A: Heysel to Hermann Debroux.
   1B: Bizet to Stockel.
   Line 2: Circle line from Simonis to Clémenceau.
   Pré-Métro: from Gare du Nord to Gare du Midi and Albert.

● For information on the metro, trams and buses in Brussels, contact STIB/MIVB ✉ 6th floor, 20 galerie de la Toison d'Or ☎ General information 02 515 2000; bus information 02 515 3064; www.stib.be.

● One-way tickets are available at metro stations, from bus or tram drivers or at newsagents with the STIB sign. Special tickets are available at metro stations or from the tourist office in Grand' Place. A ticket is valid for one hour on a bus, tram or metro. You must get the ticket stamped on the bus/tram or in the metro station.

BUSES IN BRUGES

● Although this guide gives bus numbers for every sight, the heart of the city is small and it is easy to walk everywhere. However, the efficient bus network makes it easy to explore farther afield.

● Buy tickets on board or from newsstands (in which case you must get them stamped on the bus). A one-day pass *(dagticket)* is available.

● Information line ☎ 059 56 53 53.

TRAINS

● Brussels has three main stations: Gare du Midi/Zuidstation, Gare Centrale/Centraal Station and Gare du Nord/Noordstation. Two other stations, Schumann and Quartier Léopold, serve the EU institutions and the headquarters of NATO. Bruges has only one station, near the heart of the city.

● Tickets are sold in stations, not on the train. Special offers are available on weekends and for day trips.

● Frequent trains from central Brussels run to the outlying areas and from Bruges to the coast.

● Train information: SNCB/NMBS ☎ 02 528 2828 (Brussels); 050 38 23 82 (Bruges); www.b-rail.be.

STUDENTS

Reductions are available on ticket prices for all state-run museums for holders of recognized international student cards.

METRO OFFERS

● The most economical way to travel by Brussels public transport is to buy ten tickets *(dix trajets)*, 5 tickets *(cinq trajets)* or a 12-hour unlimited travel pass, all valid on bus, tram or metro. You must get the ticket stamped on the bus/tram or in the metro station.

● You can buy a Brussels Card from the tourist office on the Grand' Place for €30. This includes all travel for 72 hours on public transport, a city map, free entry to some museums and reductions in certain shops, restaurants and exhibitions.

Essential Facts

BRUGES MUSEUMS

All the Bruges museums (www.museabrugge.be), except the privately owned ones, close on Monday.

MONEY

The euro is the official currency of Belgium. Bank notes in come in denominations of 5, 10, 20, 50, 100, 200 and 500 euros and coins in denominations of 1, 2, 5, 10, 20 and 50 cents and 1 and 2 euros.

10 euros

50 euros

200 euros

500 euros

LOST/STOLEN PROPERTY

● Report stolen property to the police. For insurance purposes, always ask for a certificate of loss.

● Brussels' central police station is on rue du Marché au Charbon (☎ 02 517 9611).

● Lost Property offices for public transport are at: Porte de Namur metro station, next to Press Shop, Brussels ☎ 02 515 2394; 7 Hauwerstraat, Bruges ☎ 050 44 88 44.

MAIL

● Stamps are available from post offices and vending machines.

● Brussels Central Post Office is at 1E/F avenue Fosny, next to the Gare du Midi (☎ 02 524 4308 ◉ 7am–11pm).

● Bruges Post Office is at 5 Markt (☎ 050 33 14 11 ◉ Mon–Fri 9.30–5, Sat 9.30–1).

MEDICAL TREATMENT

● ▷ 116 for details of the European Health Insurance Card.

● Standards of medical care are high. Most doctors speak French and English and will visit if you are too sick to visit their offices. Visits must be paid for in cash or by cheque. The following hospitals provide 24-hour emergency assistance:

MEDICAL TREATMENT IN BRUSSELS

● Hôpital Universitaire St.-Luc, Wolune St.-Lambert ✉ 10 avenue d'Hippocrate ☎ 02 764 1111

● Hôpital St-Pierre ✉ 322 rue Haute ☎ 02 535 3111

● Hôpital Universitaire des Enfants Reine Fabiola (for children) ✉ 15 avenue Jean Crocq, Laeken ☎ 02 477 3100

MEDICAL TREATMENT IN BRUGES

● Akademisch Ziekenhuis Sint-Jan Te Brugge ✉ Ruddershave 10 ☎ 050 45 21 11

● Algemeen Ziekenhuis Sint-Lucas ✉ Campus St.-Lucas, St.-Lucaslaan 29 ☎ 050 36 91 11

MEDICINES
● Pharmacies *(Pharmacie/Apotheek)*, marked with a green cross, open Mon–Fri 9–6. Each displays a list of pharmacies that open outside these hours.

NEWSPAPERS
● Newspapers include the Flemish *De Morgen* and *De Standaard* and the French-language *Le Soir*.

SENSIBLE PRECAUTIONS
● By law, visitors over 21 must carry a passport or ID card at all times.
● Watch out for pickpockets and bag-snatchers in crowded areas in Brussels and at stations.
● In Brussels, take a taxi at night, rather than the metro, bus or tram.
● Be careful in downtown Brussels, especially the red-light area at Gare du Nord, which can be dangerous at night, and the area near Comte de Flandre metro station, which is known for street crime.

SMOKING
● Smoking is banned in public places, but allowed in restaurants, which now increasingly have no-smoking areas.

TELEPHONES
● Many phone booths accept only prepaid phone cards, available from post offices, supermarkets, stations and newsstands.
● International calls are expensive. Rates are slightly lower 8pm–8am and on Sunday.
● The city codes (☎ 02 for Brussels; 050 for Bruges) must be used even when calling from within the city.
● To call the UK from Belgium dial 00 44, then drop the first 0 from the area code. To call Belgium from the UK dial 00 32, then drop the first 0 from the area code.
● To call the US from Belgium dial 001. To call Belgium from the US dial 011 32, then drop the first 0 from the area code.

EMERGENCY TELEPHONE NUMBERS
Ambulance/fire ☎ 100
Police ☎ 101

Brussels doctors on emergency call ☎ 02 479 1818; www.mgbru.be

Bruges doctors on emergency call 🕙 Fri–Mon 8am–8pm ☎ 050 81 38 99

General emergency ☎ 112
24hr Red Cross ambulance ☎ 105

TOILETS
Public toilets are usually clean. Tip attendants in bigger restaurants and cafés; the amount is posted on the wall.

NEED TO KNOW ESSENTIAL FACTS

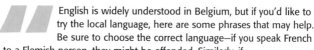

Language

English is widely understood in Belgium, but if you'd like to try the local language, here are some phrases that may help. Be sure to choose the correct language—if you speak French to a Flemish person, they might be offended. Similarly, if you speak Flemish to a French-speaking *Bruxellois,* they may well reply in French with some disdain.

BASIC VOCABULARY (FRENCH)

Oui/Non	Yes/no
S'il vous plaît	Please
Merci	Thank you
Excusez-moi	Excuse me
Bonjour	Hello
Au revoir	Goodbye
Parlez-vous anglais?	Do you speak English?
Je ne comprends pas	I don't understand
Combien?	How much?
Où est/sont...?	Where is/are...?
Ici/là	Here/there
Tournez à gauche/ droite	Turn left/right
Tout droit	Straight on
Quand?	When?
Aujourd'hui	Today
Hier	Yesterday
Demain	Tomorrow
Combien de temps?	How long?
À quelle heure ouvrez/fermez-vous?	What time do you open/close?
Avez vous...?	Do you have...?
Une chambre simple	A single room
Une chambre double	A double room
Avec salle de bains	With bathroom
Le petit déjeuner	Breakfast
Le déjeuner	Lunch
Le dîner	Dinner
Acceptez-vous des cartes de credit?	Do you accept credit cards?
J'ai besoin d'un médecin/dentiste	I need a doctor/ dentist
Pouvez-vous m'aider?	Can you help me?
Où est l'hôpital?	Where is the hospital?
Où est le commissariat?	Where is the police station?

NUMBERS (FRENCH)

un	1
deux	2
trois	3
quatre	4
cinq	5
six	6
sept	7
huit	8
neuf	9
dix	10
onze	11
douze	12
treize	13
quatorze	14
quinze	15
seize	16
dix-sept	17
dix-huit	18
dix-neuf	19
vingt	20

CONVERSATION (FLEMISH)

Ja/neen	Yes/no
Alstublieft	Please
Dank u	Thank you
Excuseer	Excuse me
Hallo	Hello
Goeiemorgen	Good morning
Goeienavond	Good evening
Tot ziens	Goodbye
Spreekt u Engels?	Do you speak English?
Ik begrijp u niet	I don't understand

USEFUL QUESTIONS (FLEMISH)

Hoeveel?	How much?
Waar is/ zijn…?	Where is/are…?
Wanneer?	When?
Hoelang?	How long?
Wanneer is het open/ gesloten?	At what time do you open/close?
Heeft u…?	Do you have…?
Hoeveel kost dit?	How much is this?
Aanvaard u een kredietkaart?	Do you take credit cards?
Kunt u mij helpen?	Can you help me?
Waar is het zieken huis/politie kantoor?	Where is the hospital/ police station?

WORDS AND PHRASES (FLEMISH)

Hier	Here
Daar	There
Sla rechts af	Turn right
Sla links af	Turn left
Rechtdoor	Straight
Een enkele kamer	A single room
Een dubbele kamer	A double room
Met/zonder badkamer	With/without a bathroom
Ik heb een dokter/ tandarts nodig	I need a doctor/ dentist

NUMBERS (FLEMISH)

een	1
twee	2
drie	3
vier	4
vijf	5
zes	6
zeven	7
acht	8
negen	9
tien	10
elf	11
twaalf	12
dertien	13
veertien	14
vijftien	15
zestien	16
zeventien	17
achttien	18
negentien	19
twintig	20
een en twintig	21
dertig	30
veertig	40
vijftig	50
zestig	60
zeventig	70
tachtig	80
negentig	90
honderd	100
duizend	1,000

WHEN? (FLEMISH)

Vandaag	Today
Gisteren	Yesterday
Morgen	Tomorrow
Ontbijt	Breakfast
Lunch	Lunch
Diner/ avondeten	Dinner

Timeline

EARLY DAYS

- Brocsella (Brussels) was first mentioned in AD695 on the trade route between Cologne and Flanders.
- In 979, Charles, Duke of Lorraine, moved to St.-Géry (central Brussels), founding the city.
- In 1459 Philip the Good, having inherited Flanders and Burgundy, brought Brabant and Holland under his control and settled in Brussels.

BRUSSELS

1515 Charles V, soon to be Holy Roman Emperor and King of Spain and the Netherlands, arrives in the city and stays until he abdicates in 1555.

1568 A revolt begins that leads to the independence of the United Province of the Netherlands from Spain, but not of present-day Belgium, which becomes known as the Spanish Netherlands.

1695 French forces attack Brussels, destroying 4,000 buildings.

1713–94 Brussels is capital of the Austrian Netherlands, under Hapsburg rule.

1795 Brussels is under French rule.

1815 Brussels reverts to the Dutch, after Napoleon Bonaparte's defeat at Waterloo.

1830 The Belgian Revolution leads to independence in January 1831.

1957 Brussels becomes the HQ of the EEC.

1993 Belgium becomes a federal state.

2002 Euro notes and coins are introduced.

2006 The balance of power tips in favour of the Socialists at local elections.

From left to right: Napoleon; a map showing the positions of the British and French armies at the Battle of Waterloo; Europe Day celebrations in Brussels; Charles V; a man in medieval dress

BRUGES

AD300 Bryggja is established, named for a key bridge.

1127 The first walls go up around Bruges.

1302 Flemish craftsmen and peasants defeat a French army at the Battle of the Golden Spurs.

1468 Charles the Bold, Duke of Burgundy and son of Philip the Good, marries Margaret of York in Damme.

1488 An uprising against Archduke Maximilian, the Hapsburg heir who tried to limit the city's privileges, leads to his kidnap and three months' detention in Bruges. The reprisals against the Bruges burghers begin the steady decline of the city when Maximilian becomes emperor in 1493.

1898 Flemish is officially recognized as the country's joint language with French.

2000 Bruges becomes a Unesco World Heritage Site.

2002 The Concertgebouw opens, putting Bruges at the forefront of Flanders' cultural life.

2007 Filming begins of the British movie *In Bruges,* by Martin McDonagh. The plot revolves around two hit men who end up in the city.

TRADING SUCCESS

By the early 14th century Bruges had become one of the world's great trading cities. In 1384 Philip the Bold, Duke of Burgundy, inherited Flanders and ushered in a period of prosperity and great cultural and political changes. However, the city began to decline when Maximilian became emperor in 1493. In 1516 Genoese and Florentine traders, who had set up business ventures in Bruges under a treaty of 1395, moved to Antwerp. A further difficulty arose in 1550, when Bruges lost access to the sea, with the silting up of what is now known as the Zwin.

Index

CITYPACK TOP 25
Brussels and Bruges

WRITTEN BY Anthony Sattin and Sylvie Franquet
DESIGN CONCEPT AND DESIGN WORK Kate Harling
COVER DESIGN Jackie Bailey
INDEXER Marie Lorimer
IMAGE RETOUCHING AND REPRO Michael Moody
EDITOR Kathryn Glendenning
SERIES EDITOR Paul Mitchell

© AUTOMOBILE ASSOCIATION DEVELOPMENTS LIMITED 2007

First published 1997
Colour separation by Keenes
Printed and bound by Leo, China
A CIP catalogue record for this book is available from the British Library.

ISBN 978-0-7495-5244-2

Published by AA Publishing, a trading name of Automobile Association Developments Limited, whose registered office is Fanum House, Basing View, Basingstoke, Hampshire RG21 4EA. Registered number 1878835.

A03143
Maps in this title produced from:
  mapping © MAIRDUMONT/Falk Verlag 2007
  mapping © ISTITUTO GEOGRAFICO DE AGOSTINI S.p.A., NOVARA - 2006
Transport map © Communicarta Ltd, UK